# INEQUALITY

# INEQUALITY

The evidence of the Transport and General Workers' Union to the Royal Commission on the Distribution of Income and Wealth

SPOKESMAN BOOKS

**TGWU EVIDENCE TO ROYAL COMMISSION ON DISTRIBUTION OF INCOME AND WEALTH**

In late 1974 the Royal Commission on the Distribution of Income and Wealth invited both the Transport and General Workers' Union (TGWU) and the Trade Union Research Unit at Ruskin College, Oxford (TURU), among many other bodies, to present evidence under its "Standing Reference" and its "Income from Companies and its Distribution" Reference, and subsequently under its "Higher Incomes from Employment" Reference. It was agreed that evidence under this last Reference should be co-ordinated through the TUC, but at the initiative of its General Secretary, Jack Jones, the TGWU commissioned the assistance of the TURU in the preparation of evidence under the first two References. Papers provided by TURU formed the basis of the evidence which was developed and subsequently presented by Jack Jones and the TGWU Research Officer, Bob Harrison. This book represents the final version, which was presented to the Royal Commission early in 1975, supplemented by statements and further oral evidence from Jack Jones. A summary of the oral sessions is contained in the official Royal Commission publication of evidence, due to appear shortly.

Several people were involved in the research under the guidance of Jack Jones and Bob Harrison: John Hughes, the Director of the TURU; TURU Research Officer, Roy Moore (who edited the evidence); TURU Research Assistants Robin Beddoe and Brian Bolton; and Chris Trinder, of the Department of Economics at the University of Essex.

Published by the Bertrand Russell Peace Foundation Ltd., Bertrand Russell House, Gamble Street, Nottingham, NG7 4ET for *Spokesman Books 1976.*



Printed by the Russell Press Limited, Nottingham.

# Contents

# PART ONE

## Evidence on Income From Companies and its Distribution

# Statement by Jack Jones

## Company Incomes

Mr Chairman:

We welcome this opportunity to support and perhaps clarify the written evidence we have submitted to you on "Company Incomes". Our views on this reference must be seen as part of our total approach to the distribution of income and wealth, which we will develop when we have the opportunity to discuss the "Standing Reference" with you.

Our written evidence on Company Incomes is necessarily lengthy and detailed. We accepted the need to analyse and comment upon the points which the government requested the Commission to report on, and the subjects of the headings under which you requested evidence.

Therefore, a considerable amount of research was necessary to determine the true facts of the various aspects of Company Incomes, and to verify the statistics which prompted our conclusions. But these conclusions are now clear, and today we bring them to your attention, on behalf of our membership.

This membership of ours is the most representative cross-section of the working population of this country. The distribution of incomes and wealth is of fundamental importance to our members because it determines their standard of living — not only their earnings, but their security, and the sort of society they live in. Any misrepresentation of income and wealth, any fault in their measurement, any unfairness in the way they are taxed, must be revealed and corrected if we are to achieve economic justice for our members.

So, to us, this is no academic exercise. We want to involve our membership, and the public, in this opportunity to move towards a massive redistribution of incomes and wealth. We want to see, in practice, that which most of us preach, about fair shares and equality of opportunity.

We look to you, the Royal Commission, to realise the vital importance of your terms of reference to the workers of this country, and the quality of their lives. You have a unique opportunity to bring the facts to the people. Only the facts, and all the facts, can produce the climate for real social justice.

Company incomes are a crucial aspect of distribution of income and wealth. Yet to the great majority of people they are shrouded in mystery. The jargon about shares and dividends, capital gains and depreciation, has tended to cloud the issue. The ordinary worker is taxed on his earnings. His earnings are exactly known, and he must specifically and accurately declare any additional income. His allowances for certain expenditure are clearly stipulated. Our evidence indicates that income derived from companies is not so strictly defined, and is not made accountable to the Inland Revenue with the exactitude required of our typical wage earning member.

*Ownership of Shares (Section 2)*

All forms of income, and the wealth which creates income, must in our opinion, be brought into the analysis of the matter – and into the system of taxation. Consideration of the Ownership of Shares (our Section 2) is basic to this assessment or definition of economic power. Any increase in the value of any individual's property, increases his command over resources. So ownership of shares gives a direct source of incomes; title to wealth which is very likely to appreciate; and a degree of control over the distribution of profit and other decisions which determine future income. The dividends received (only 25% of the level of undistributed profits in 1974) are of small importance compared to this command of assets which reflect not only retained income, but also the value of the whole community's investment in capital assets and services.

Our figures show the remarkable concentration of this economic power – nearly 93% of all securities and shares being held by 5.3% of the total population over 15 years of age. The compounding of this power by interlocking relationships is not difficult to demonstrate. There is no evidence of any lessening of this concentration.

The switch in share ownership from personal holdings to institutional portfolios in the last two decades has not meant any significant dispersal of the dividend income, the wealth-aspects represented by shares, or the control of the corporate bodies. Some of the movement has been into insurance and pension funds, and investment trusts, but banks, nominee companies, and non-financial companies have also attracted some of the share formerly in personal holdings. And the benefit derived from these insurance, pension, and investment funds – with the controlling influence described – flows in the main to the same groups of people who own the personal holdings: very little income is diverted to the mass of working people. The myths of democratising the financial power-structure through the use of pension funds must be exposed. It is still the directors and senior staff who benefit most.

*Nature of Equity Shareholding (Section 3)*

The enormous importance of this concentration of income, wealth, and direct economic power derived from the "Ownership of Shares", led us to consider the Nature and Function of Equity Shareholding, in Section 3. Our members earning a wage on the shop floor are led by employers to belive that the Equity Shareholding Function is vital to attract the investment necessary to keep them in jobs. This Function provided 5% of industry's investment funds in only one of the last eight years – in two of these years it induced less than 1% of the total. Equity Capital issues are only of marginal importance in financing real capital formation – so what is its real function? These pieces of paper are the key to the take-over and merger activities by which the owners seek to enlarge and strengthen their controlling influence. Such take-overs are likely to be directed by commercial need to improve or defend the value of existing assets – which may mean shutting down or reducing production capacity. The risk inherent in such activity to our members is obvious. And they do not stand to gain any income or wealth for such manipulations.

"Risk" is still advanced as a justification for this privileged concentration of wealth and power in the company incomes sector. Even though equity now produces very little additional capital, it may be held that the risk run by the owners, the possibility of loss, entitles them to their considerable accretions of income and wealth. But, no – the risk element, as with the alleged function, of equity capital, does not stand-up under analysis. Our evidence is that the real capital value of equity shares has steadily improved over the last 50 years up to 1968 – recent fluctuations in stock market prices have shown a most remarkable resurgence in the last two months.

Other developments minimising any risk element are the increasing influence of multi-product and multi-national firms in the economy: and it should be remembered that the risks have been concentrated in the property and financial sectors where speculation has been common.

Other ordinary share dealings have been very important in acquisitions and mergers – serving the financial strategy of the share-owners, often by creating real risks for the men and women employed in the units to be reorganised. The degree of concentration of ownership serves to reduce the potential risk in equity share-holding.

The great role and value of public money (through investments grants etc.) in supporting private capital and company incomes, cannot be ignored. The value of private assets was protected by over £3,000m from the state in 1970-74.

We would argue that with the lessening of competitive restraints due to take-overs, etc., price control is a necessary check on the ability of share-holders to build up the value of shares by administered pricing policies.

There is no evidence at all to sustain a belief that to take away Dividend Controls would attract a higher level of real capital formation.

Nor does there appear to be any evidence to indicate that the change to the imputation system of corporation tax, which will lower taxation on distributed dividends, will have any effect on increasing real investment funds. There should be no indiscriminate encouragement to higher levels of profit distribution – particularly in our present need of investment. The 1965 Corporation Tax would seem to have produced a more desirable response, with more favourable treatment of retained profits.

Any tax favours to the owners of share capital, at a time when the tax burden on ordinary workers is increasing, will militate against acceptance of the restraint being requested as necessary to deal with the perils of inflation. *(Section 2 of Standing Reference Evidence)*

This matter of "privilege" within the taxation system led us to examine the position of "Wealthy Shareholders", in Section 4.

*Privileged Tax Position of Wealthy Shareholders (Section 4)*

We considered Section 4 of our evidence to you ("The Privileged Tax Position of Wealthy Shareholders") to be of the greatest practical importance at the present time. In consequence, and in the light of the information we collated showing that companies were turning over *en masse* to the issue of scrip dividends, we also emphasised strongly within the Trades Union Congress the urgency of the need to remove the tax privileged treatment of scrip dividends.

The Royal Commission will, of course, be aware that The Government has announced in a written reply in the House of Commons that as from 6th April 1975 such stock dividends will be subject to progressive taxation under proposals that it will bring forward in the next Budget. The recipient of stock dividends will be chargeable to higher rate income tax and to the investment income surcharge on the amount of the dividend "grossed up" at the basic rate of tax. The TGWU not only fully supports this important step by The Government;

we consider that it was absolutely essential in order to maintain the respect for social justice without which the element of restraint involved in the Social Contract cannot work.

But the fact that The Government has now acted vigorously and correctly on this matter to restore the basis of progressive taxation does not mean that we should immediately pass on to other subjects. It is important to understand what was at issue.

First of all this episode of "scrip dividends" demonstrated the very relevant point that what might look like a minor technical clause in a Finance Act dealing with an aspect of company income could effectively abolish the progressive income tax system so far as wealthy shareholders were concerned. Regardless of their marginal tax rate (which in some cases must be 98% and in many cases must be over 80%), shareholders given the "scrip" option were in effect subject to no more than standard rate taxation and then eventual liability to the 30% Capital Gains tax. This kind of erosion of the progressive tax base must never be allowed to happen again.

Secondly, this experience demonstrates that it is not possible to brush aside such concerns by assuming that the "loophole" is only a small one. What started as a trickle of companies recognising the nature of the 1973 Finance Act's clause on "scrip" became a stream and then a torrent. After our first submission of evidence to you, we made a search through thousands of company records. We found that already by mid-February 1,970 companies had adopted scrip dividend options. What is more, if the largest companies – with £20 million or more equity capitalisation – were examined, already companies with a total capitalisation (for equity) of over £3,500 million had gone over to scrip issues. After our search more companies announced their adoption of scrip issues virtually every day. Indeed, on the very day of the government announcement ICI itself announced that it was going to develop a system of stock issues. In other words, our estimate to you that if the system became general the tax loss would mount well above £100 million, and possibly over £200 million, was rapidly becoming true.

Thirdly, this demonstrates the crucial point that for social justice *all* forms of income and wealth distribution must be brought into the reckoning. Hence the special importance of the continuing investigatory role of this Royal Commission. In 1973 we had a government that under the slogan of "felt fairness" held down the wages of millions of low paid workers by a statutory incomes policy while, with the other hand so to speak, their Finance Act of the same year launched the "scrip dividend" on its way. We know what to think of the dishonesty of such a government. We learn also that the trade unions, as representative of the great mass of workers, must extend their views on income priorities and tax systems to every aspect of the distribution of wealth.

Fourthly, so far as we have been able to discover very few of the business and financial groups that have provided evidence to this Royal Commission on company income found the crucial issues presented by scrip dividends worthy of mention. Our academic friends tell us that in research a "negative finding" may be an important one. This is a case of the dog that didn't bark. Why was it that so few institutions close to the city and business felt that this was a matter that should be brought out into the open? Why was our evidence, so far as we have been able to find out, somewhat unique in the emphasis it gave to this matter? We are forced to conclude that not all the bodies giving evidence to you on this matter have firmly at heart the basic principles of progressive taxation, of basing tax upon ability to pay. Not all of them, perhaps, understand that we are living in an economy in which all forms of income and wealth have got to be openly and honestly examined, and felt to be socially accountable. Pay determination has been out in the open for a long time with the glare of publicity directed to it. It is for this Royal Commission to see that the searchlight of public accountability is turned also on the wealthy, and on the operations of our corporate sector.

Public Accountability also must be asserted in the matter of the determining of the "true" profit. Our members cannot juggle with the figures on which they are taxed. They are entitled to the assurance that company incomes will be similarly treated.

*Trends in Company Income – Problems of Measurement and Control (Section 1)*

For any serious examination of company income and its distribution it is necessary therefore to seek to establish what recent trends have been. This leads to some serious problems of interpretation of statistics, of definitions, and measurement. Of course, inflation has added to the problems of measurement and the area of disagreement. Consequently, Section 1 of our evidence was by its nature fairly technical. Essentially what we have tried to do is to draw attention to a whole series of ways in which a distorted view of company profits within the national product may arise. We have also looked in a preliminary way at the contrast between the relative lightening of the tax burden on companies as compared with the long period trend to tax earned income more heavily.

On all these matters there are no easy answers as to what is the "right" way to view the measurement of company income. The long time it has taken the Sandilands Committee to work on the question of inflation accounting makes that clear. It is our hope that the Royal Commission will take a continuing interest in analysis in this field, and will seek to overcome deficiencies in the material currently available.

Since we submitted our evidence we have noticed reports of one study which we think would be worth more detailed consideration by the Royal Commission. It certainly appears to offer a corrective to those commentators who arrive at the conclusion that company profitability has shrunk drastically as a result of stock appreciation and higher replacement costs of equipment having to be taken into account.

Phillips and Drew, in their February 1975 "Market Review" (pages 2 to 3), refer to a detailed study of theirs in which they applied "current purchasing power" (CPP) inflation accounting to a sample of 116 leading companies. We are not suggesting that this method of measurement is in all senses the "right" one – but it has been strongly advanced by the accountancy profession and what Phillips and Drew draw attention to is very important.

They emphasise that adjusting for stock appreciation (i.e. deducting the amount by which stock values have risen over a period) is only *one* part of inflation accounting. The others are the increase in depreciation charge, and the adjustment for the fall in the real value of the company's net borrowing. They then show the adjustments called for by inflation accounting on the 1973 accounts, as a percentage change on pre-tax profits:-

*Depreciation* reduces pre-tax profits by 15%
*Stock Appreciation* reduces pre-tax profits by 12½%
*The Gain on Net Monetary Liabilities* increases pre-tax profits by 22½%
*Other adjustments* increase pre-tax profits by 5%.

Overall, the net effect of these pluses and minuses is no more than a 5% fall in pre-tax profits on "inflation accounting" rules as compared with the conventional historical accounts. What is more, Phillips and Drew calculate that for the 1974 accounts of these companies the pluses and minuses cancel out completely and

> "CPP (current purchasing power) profits were probably no lower than conventional profits in 1974".

These commentators then go on to make the important points:-

> "The UK company taxation system can now be regarded as, if anything, *over-generous* (Phillips and Drew emphasise this word), since it gives some allowance both for stock appreciation and for additional depreciation of fixed assets, by permitting many types of capital expenditure to be completely written off in the first year, without making any adjustment for the offsetting gain in the net monetary position. The consequence is that many companies now have a mini-

mal UK tax charge apart from the advance corporation tax associated with their dividend payments."

We think this is a very important conclusion. It comes, of course, from a leading City firm whose studies of pay trends have recently been treated very seriously and quoted by leading members of the government. And nobody has suggested that the taxation falling on workers' pay is now "too generous".

Closely linked to the need for a system which will openly and accurately calculate the true level of profit, is the need for much more meaningful provision of information by companies.

*Provision of Information By Companies (Section 5)*

Knowledge of the real level of Company Incomes must be verified by public access to the information on all matters of concern.

We support the views of both the last Conservative Government, and the Labour Party, which would require regulation of insider dealings: disclosure of nominee shareholdings; disclosure of directors' interests; up-to-date filing of accounts; regular statements of the flow of funds; and full information on transactions between companies, subsidiaries, etc.

But our considerable experience in dealing with disclosure of information problem in collective bargaining leads us to require much more than this. We must have standardised accounting procedures enforced which require accuracy and consistency in the valuation of such things as depreciation and stocks. The margins for error and estimation must be minimised.

The hard won experience of our members also justifies our claim that minimum statutory obligation to disclose should also be applied to the key areas of Manpower, Production, Financial Position, Investment, Sales, Profits, and 'Balance of Payments" for all companies including multi-nationals. These matters both determine, and are determined by Company Incomes policy.

*Conclusion*

Mr. Chairman, we have followed the guidelines of your Commission in this analysis of Company Incomes. Our evidence clearly indicates urgent matters of concern in this aspect of the Distribution of Wealth and Incomes.

Our policy is that all forms of Incomes and Wealth must be clearly brought into an increasingly *Progressive* system of taxation. We believe we have shown in this evidence that much of the Income and Wealth derived from Companies cannot be subjected to this principle because they are not properly identified, valued, or accounted for.

We look to the Commission to take due account of the interest and concern of our members, and devise a means of making Company Incomes as accountable as are the earnings of shop floor workers.

*Companies with equity capitalisation of over £100 million that went over to the "scrip dividend" option:*

| | *Equity Capitalisation (£ million)* |
|---|---|
| Allied Breweries | 279 |
| B.I.C.C. | 165 |
| Brooke Bond Liebig | 116 |
| E.M.I. | 625 |
| G.K.N. | 345 |
| Marks and Spencer | 171 |
| S. Pearson | 114 |
| Pilkington Bros. | 158 |
| J. Sainsbury | 111 |
| Thorn Electrical | 180 |
| U.D.S. Group | 158 |

# Introduction

The submission of evidence takes note of the fact that the "Company Income" reference specifically raises the question of *dividend distribution* policy. But the evidence is also concerned to encourage the *wider review* of company income that is implied by the title of the current reference.

In the very short time that has been given for submission of evidence it has not been possible to be fully comprehensive. Consequently, where studies have been made in depth by other agencies we have provided references rather than repeating in detail what is readily available elsewhere.

What the evidence concentrates on are aspects of the subject that are of major importance at this stage in the development of the current work and future research programmes of the Royal Commission. Beyond that we have tried to bear in mind the urgency arising from the current economic and social context of this inquiry. On this we have in mind not only the relationships between company profitability and financial requirements and the need to sustain the level of productive investment. We are also conscious that the current attention being paid to equitable and socially responsible policies on pay and prices must also demand an equal concern with social priorities in the approach to company income, to the tax systems applied to it, and to the distribution of dividends.

The main sections of our evidence are produced as separate papers. They cover the following ground.

*Section 1:* "Trends in Company Income – Problems of Measurement and Interpretation" recognises that the Royal Commission needs to give attention to the difficult question as to what have been the *trends* in company income over recent years. The TGWU is particularly concerned that many of the studies of data that have been put forward have been inadequate and misleading. In particular certain interested parties have juggled with presentation so as to present an exaggerated picture of a dangerously declining rate of profit. *Section 1* of our evidence concentrates therefore on a step by step study of the problems of measurement and presentation of profit trends which the Royal Commission needs to consider.

One important aspect of this is that the tax system has provided increasingly generous treatment of depreciation, while investment grants and other aid has further reduced the level of *net* taxation. The latest budget has, of course, taken this further (for tax liabilities relating to company operations in 1973/74) by an estimated £775 million reduction in taxation due to the new treatment of stock appreciation. The easing of the burden of taxation on companies over the last decade or more is shown to contrast sharply with the increased severity of direct and indirect taxation of working class income.

*Section 2:* "The Ownership of Shares" sets share ownership in the economic context of income and wealth distribution, and describes the distribution patterns of individual and institutional shareholders. The picture that emerges is of a dual inequality: the degree of concentration of personal shareholding is overwhelming; and the development of institutional shareholding has brought with it a second tendency towards reinforcing inequality. This is particularly true of pension funds, which are limited in accessibility and unequal in provisions.

*Section 3:* "The Nature of Equity Shareholding" places the current financial crisis in a wider and longer-term perspective, and identifies those factors tending to dilute the elements of risk involved in equities. The minimal role of equities in providing new company funds is contrasted with their substantial role in financing take-over activity. We conclude that employees of companies and their communities are often exposed to a greater degree of risk than shareholders. Serious doubts are also raised as to the replacement of the preferable 1965 Corporation Tax with the 1973 Imputation System.

*Section 4:* "The Privileged Tax Position of Wealthy Shareholders" is concerned with the manifest unfairness apparent in the minimisation of taxation liability arising from companies' increasing practice of offering shares in lieu of dividend payments.

Finally, *Section 5:* "Provision of Information by Companies" identifies a host of key areas which are inadequately covered by statutory obligations for the disclosure of company information. More information and accountability is required in all these areas if a true and comprehensive picture of income from companies is to be obtained.

The main sections of our evidence show *both* the need for more and better information in order to improve the democratic accountability of the company system *and* the fact that behind the structure of company income and its taxation and distribution there are multiple elements of inequity and marked inequality.

For the *immediate* needs of the economy and the people who work in it we would emphasise:-

a) "Institutional" saving should be channelled more directly into financing the future *real* investment (capital formation) of the community, and not merely into trading in existing "equity" claims.

b) A substantial proportion of *undistributed* company income should be treated for what it really is, as wealth created by – and responsible to – the whole working community, and not as wealth directly swelling the real value of existing equity capital.

c) The system of company taxation should revert to the 1965 type of Corporation Tax, away from the "imputation" model which is effectively lowering total taxation falling on distributed dividends.

d) The right of shareholders to receive a scrip issue in lieu of income from dividends should be removed, as it is a blatant example of encouragement of tax avoidance on behalf of those with high incomes.

e) In the current state of the economy we do not think that loosening the restraints on dividend distribution generally would help companies with the finance of maintained real investment programmes. We have to recognise the priority in national policy that has to be given to companies:-

- maintaining or increasing their real investment;
- maintaining or increasing their net exports;
- co-operating with recognised trade unions in socially responsible manpower planning.

It is only in so far as companies are pursuing such economically and socially responsible policies that it becomes reasonable to increase the freedom they may enjoy as to dividend distribution policy.

# 1

# Trends in Company Income - Problems of Measurement & Interpretation

Any serious review by the Royal Commission of the question not merely of dividend distribution but more widely of company income cannot avoid the controversy over *trends in company income* in recent years. There are in fact a number of severe problems that are encountered in attempting to assess realistically what these trends are. By careful selection of base dates, and avoidance of qualifications that have to be made about particular published series, it is possible to present a very exaggerated picture of the fall in company profitability in the UK. Misunderstandings as to the real trends that have been developing may give a wrong direction to policy measures. For instance a false view of profitability may lead to "remedy" by way of exaggerated reduction in the contribution that companies make via taxation to wider community needs. Or it may lead to a deliberate weakening of the criteria of statutory price controls, thus inviting an accelerated rate of inflation – with all the damaging consequences that this may entail.

It is certainly not possible at this stage to give a definitive account of profit and profitability trends, or to provide an analysis of major aspects of company income that would not be challenged from some interest group or researcher. But it is clearly the responsibility of the Royal Commission to recognise the main areas of inadequate information and of controversy in interpretation and seek to develop positive research and improvement of existing sources so that the areas of doubt and ignorance are reduced in the future.

This paper attempts to indicate some of the factors which are often neglected, and some of the apparently simple methods of measurement which in fact conceal complexities that may sharply alter our perceptions.

### *Cyclical Movements*

Year to year comparisons can be misleading in view of the sensitivity of company profits and profitability to changing rates of capacity utilisation and the rigour of product market competition in the course of the trade cycle. Of course the emphasis on seeking comparisons with *equivalent points* in successive trade cycles, in order to avoid the distortion when non-equivalent years are compared, still involves some element of uncertainty. Thus 1973, as a "peak" trade cycle year can best be compared with the year 1964 as the "peak" year two trade cycles earlier. The expansion phase of the cycle in the late 1960s was particularly short and governmental policy intervened to deflate demand (late in 1968 and in 1969) so that no "peak" year closely equivalent to either 1964 or 1973 emerged.

This might seem an elementary consideration, but considerable attention was paid to allegedly falling profitability in the later 1960s and particularly 1970 (e.g. by the CBI, by the Treasury in its memorandum to the Wilberforce Committee of Inquiry early in 1971, and by academic researchers such as Glyn and Sutcliffe) with quite inadequate emphasis on the trade cycle context.

More analysis would be desirable on the relationship between changes in various components of company income and various measures of profitability in relation to specific stages in successive trade cycles; this is more complex than it might seem given both elements of differentiation in different trade cycles and the operation of lagged relationships in the course of the cycle. (Thus the turning point of fixed capital formation is generally markedly later than that for cycles of durable production or business stocks; considerable additions to the capital stock become available in the middle of the "stagnation" or "recession" phase of the cycle. Not only is profitability adversely affected at this point, but companies may also seek to raise profitability by closures and disposals of previously productive assets. In fact, much of this search for increased short run profit – or loss elimination – may be breaking up valuable teams of workers and technical staff, creating future imbalance and curtailing capacity which will be needed later in the expansion stage of the cycle. This was the lesson of 1971, and it is urgent to study such matters so that the wrong pattern of company response is not repeated in 1975.)

### *Multi-national Companies*

There must be increasing problems of the exact measurement of company income in relation to the UK economy as a result of the increasing shift of company structures to a "multi-national" pattern. The large multi-product and multi-national companies that dominate most of the key sectors of the economy may in a number of ways handle their intra-company transactions so that a distorted picture is presented (as compared with what would have occurred through arms-length relationships). Typically, a high proportion of exports and of imports go to or are derived from other subsidiaries or divisions of the multi-national enterprise. This immediately poses questions of "transfer pricing" and of the flexibility with which the company may choose to take higher or lower profits in different countries (depending on tax rates and other considerations). Thus if a company reports lower profits in the UK but increasing profitability in, say, its South American subsidiaries, the network of transactions involved may be highly complex. The problem of measuring costs and profits may arise also from the existence in the UK of a costly headquarters operation (which may include also central services, R & D, etc.). If all of this is allocated as cost to the UK operations a quite different picture would be presented to that involved in allocating the cost across the global operation. Similar considerations arise in seeking to obtain a real allocation of costs and revenues as a result of the national source chosen for company borrowing, and the network of internal borrowing and lending between different national subsidiaries which can be made more complex still by changes in leads and lags in payment for goods and services exchanged between the various component parts of the company.

It is important that specific attention is paid by the Royal Commission to this increasingly important dimension of the assessment of company income. For one thing, in so far as a company may be able to operate in such a way as to reduce UK profits (and receive them in some other national centre instead) it will be reducing its payments of taxation with all that that implies in terms of reduced contribution to the needs of the community – and a transfer of the burden of financing community services to other shoulders.

### *Return on Capital*

Estimation of trends in *profitability* rather than of profits raises the problem of the reliability of data on the capital stock or other aggregate chosen for purposes of comparison.

Recognition of the degree of error that may be involved is often lacking, even in serious official studies. Thus the valuable pioneering study, "Estimating companies' rate of return on capital employed" (*Economic Trends*, November 1974), is seriously defective in this respect, e.g.:-

(i) Exclusion of land and working capital in national accounts measurement of capital employed is mentioned, but the sheer unreliability of the capital stock measure is not. National

Accounts statistics have a category, "C", which represents the most unreliable estimates with a margin of error of more than 10%. It should be noted that "capital consumption" and "stock appreciation" fall into this extremely unreliable category. But for capital stock estimates a fourth category, "D", has to be developed which involves a margin of error of more than 20%. Estimates of the capital stock in "distribution and other services" fall into this category.

(ii) It is assumed that all stock appreciation can be attributed to industrial and commercial companies "since that relating to financial companies can be assumed to be negligible". Unless the definition and classification of financial companies is exceptionally pure (instead of being that their income is "derived mainly from transactions in financial assets") this assumption seems questionable.

(iii) It is not necessarily generally understood that although "property companies" are grouped with "insurance, banking, and finance", in the sections of the National Accounts statistics that are analysed by industry, they are included with industrial and commercial companies in the sectoral analysis. Given the rapidly increasing importance of property companies in the British economy in recent years, and their generally low rates of *income* in relation to capital, this may have been a factor leading to an *apparently* falling rate of return on the part of industrial and commercial companies. The outturn for the industrial and commercial sector *excluding* property companies might look somewhat different. The point at least should not have been passed over in silence.

Further problems occur if the attempt is made to move away from national accounts to estimates of capital employed that are made in company accounts. Some of the problems involved in the various possible measures of "capital employed" are set out in the article previously mentioned (*Economic Trends,* November 1974). They include variations in charging for depreciation not only as between companies but in the same company over time. Thus the widespread change to "straight line" calculations from the "declining balance" method is said (*op. cit.* page xxxi) to affect the comparison over time of profits after depreciation by lowering the figure for later years in comparison with the figure for earlier years.

### *The Share of Total Product*

It is understandable, given these difficulties, that many analysts of profitability in recent years have preferred to relate profit data to some measure of the total national product. Even here, care has to be taken as to the suitability of the aggregate that is used. For instance if emphasis is being placed on profits before depreciation and stock appreciation have been provided for then the appropriate aggregate would seem to be not the familiar gross domestic product (which is calculated *after* stock appreciation) but the somewhat awkwardly entitled aggregate "total domestic income before providing for depreciation and stock appreciation". If attention is being given to profits after providing for stock appreciation and capital consumption then the appropriate aggregate for purposes of comparison might reasonably be net domestic product (gross domestic product less capital consumption). (In 1973 "total domestic incomes" were over £3 billion more than gross domestic product, and net domestic product was over £7 billion less than GDP so that different choices of a measure of the national product can produce substantial differences in the appearance of profit comparisons.)

But this is not the only point of difficulty in attempting to relate profits series to some measure of the national product. A further serious misunderstanding can arise (not least on the part of any readers of profit analyses who are not entirely familiar with national income and expenditure accounting conventions). Simply, a series comparing company trading profits (*including* the financial company sector) with some measure of national product will show a greater apparent erosion of profitability than if the financial sector is excluded.

The conventions of national income accounting vis a vis *financial* companies are such as to show for them a large and rapidly increasing *deficit* on "gross trading profits"; this is because all management expenses are charged against this item and only bank charges, commissions, etc. offset this. The enormous income from "non-trading" income is dealt with separately. The Blue Book shows financial companies with a *deficit* on "gross trading profits" of £296 million in 1964, rising to £787 million deficit in 1973. Both the Treasury and the CBI in the past have concentrated attention on trends in the "gross trading profits" of all companies, without making it clear that on this account the part is greater than the whole, since e.g. in 1973 the "gross trading profits" of all *non*-financial companies were £787 million *more* than the published figure for the "gross trading profits" of *all* companies!

It is important, then, to avoid a misleading deflation of the share of profits arising from the deficit on gross trading profits of financial companies.

There are two ways of doing this:-

a) To concentrate on the *wider* category of "company income arising in the UK"; this includes both "gross trading profits" and the "rent and non-trading income" derived by companies from operations in the UK but received from sectors other than the company sector itself. (The national income accounting practice treats "rent and non-trading income" as a "transfer" from other sectors rather than as an addition to the national product, so this creates some problems of comparison with movements in the national product.) It is very important to understand that the "rent and non-trading income" part of total company profits has been increasing disproportionately fast over recent years; by 1973 it added over £4,000 million to company income arising in the UK. So to ignore it is to create another distortion in our understanding of the company sector. Between the boom year 1964 and the boom year 1973, for instance, company "rent and non-trading income" in the UK rose fourfold, while the national product (in current money values) increased just over twofold. The "transfer" payments from other sectors to the company sector involved in this "rent and non-trading income" rose from 3.6% of the gross domestic product to 6.7%.

b) To look more narrowly at the "gross trading profits" of industrial and commercial companies. This requires further correction if longer period comparisons are being attempted, to allow for the fact that some companies (e.g. steel) have been nationalised. It is possible to allow for this fairly accurately.*

*The Effect of Inflation*

A further area of difficulty arises from the desire to adjust estimates of profit to allow for replacement cost measurement of depreciation ("capital consumption"), and to allow also for stock appreciation. Both these represent some attempt to bring some reference to inflationary processes into the calculation of "true" profits. But there are uncertainties as to the "truth" of inflation accounting, and particularly as to the *partial* application of inflation accounting, notably the application of all aspects that substantially *deflate* estimates profit but the non-application of those aspects that would *raise* estimated profit. The lop-sidedness of

---

* National Income and Expenditure 1963-73, Table 32, contains the appropriation accounts of non-nationalised companies. As this table includes financial companies, the picture of what happened to non nationalised industrial and commercial companies has to be built up by deducting the financial company account figures from Table 32.

the approach frequently being resorted to led the City's leading firm of investment analysts to the following recent comment:-

> "We would be strongly against deducting stock appreciation in calculating profits and earnings unless this were done as part of a comprehensive inflation accounting adjustment. Deducting stock appreciation is only one of three main planks of inflation accounting, the other ones being the increase in the depreciation charge and the gain or loss (usually a substantial gain) on the net monetary position. Making either one or two of these adjustments without the third tends to give a misleadingly pessimistic picture of company profitability."
>
> – *(Phillips and Drew Research: The November Budget, 13 November 1974)*

Clearly, this misleadingly pessimistic picture is more and more frequently resorted to in recent studies, but *without* the qualification given such forceful expression by Phillips and Drew. Thus, the "rates of return" article already referred to in its Table 1, Cols. 3, 6 and 9 produces precisely such a "misleadingly pessimistic" analysis without making any reference to the partial nature of its approach (in Cols. 1 to 3 it also commits the further misleading error of an "all companies" analysis, incorporating the financial companies and their increasing deficit on gross trading profit).

Once again, estimates of stock appreciation and of capital consumption are employed without due recognition of the range of error involved. The official guide to National Accounts Statistics emphasises the "wide margin of error" involved. Considerable year to year revision of Blue Book estimates should underline that factor for both entities. Clearly data on profits expressed *after* capital consumption and *after* stock appreciation provision are markedly less reliable than the original profits figures – but this is rarely pointed out by those that pay such attention to these deductions.

Besides, the methodology, which in the case of stock appreciation includes the assumption that market prices indices can be substituted for actual prices paid during the period, may be highly suspect for instance in the special circumstances of the recent rapid rise (and for some commodities, rapid and drastic fall) in commodity prices. This suggests that a very selective and careful approach is needed; for instance in 1974 heavy falls have taken place in prices of textile fibres, rubber, and non-ferrous metals. Companies in these sectors may well have experienced extensive stock *depreciation.*

One example may indicate the methodological doubts about the treatment of stock appreciation, since it shows that prices paid by leading importers must have diverged widely from the official index price measurement of wholesale prices on the home market:-

| *Raw Cotton Prices* | *Direct Imports (1972 = 100)* | *Home Sales (1972 = 100)* |
|---|---|---|
| 1st qtr. 1973 | 97 | 115 |
| 2nd qtr. 1973 | 106 | 132 |
| 3rd qtr. 1973 | 123 | 212 |
| 4th qtr. 1973 | 160 | 242 |

Clearly an estimate of stock appreciation based on the wholesale selling prices index for cotton would have exaggerated the provision required by importing companies (it looks also as if somebody was collecting quite genuine "stock profits" by reselling imported cotton).

*Taxation*

Further serious problems of interpretation arise as a result of seeking to take into consideration, when examining trends in company income, the changing patterns and weight of taxation falling on companies (together with their receipts from subsidies such as investment grants).

The complexity of this question of the attribution of taxation to companies is made apparent in the extensive discussion on pages xxxii to xxxv of the article in the November 1974 *Economic Trends.* For instance, one method (that actually used in the article in question) would treat the standard rate of tax on dividends as part of company taxation. In a number of ways (this was certainly the spirit of the 1965 Corporation Tax) this might be seen as inappropriate and the tax on dividends might instead be viewed as falling on shareholder income instead of being measured as part of company taxation. Obviously a method that *includes* the tax on dividends as part of company taxation will make post-tax profits seem *lower* than if taxation on shareholder income is seen as something separate from taxation on companies.

Moreover, examination of Blue Book tables of company income and taxation can produce an incomplete picture. Thus investment grants are treated as a subsidy on *capital* account; in reality, in order to identify the *net* burden of taxation falling on companies it seems appropriate to deduct investment grants from the total of taxation (just as, in order to measure net indirect taxation falling on consumers, subsidies would be deducted). Moreover estimates of taxation on an "accruals" basis may be overtaken by changes in the rates of tax or allowances introduced subsequently but relating back to the year in question. Thus the November 1974 budget through its special provision for treatment of a substantial proportion of stock appreciation has produced a relief of £775 million in relation to the year 1973/4 (on tax that would have been payable in 1974/75).

Further problems arise in seeking to make comparisons as to the weight of taxation at various points in time beyond those created by major changes in tax systems. There is a problem of which entity tax should be compared with in order to show its proportion to company income. Tax is levied on total income net of interest charges. Thus the appropriate aggregate is wider than trading profits but less than "company income arising in the UK" (prior to deduction of interest charges). The Blue Book tables do indicate interest payments paid outside the company sector, so that some near approximation to the tax base seems possible.

Table I attempts to give some outline measure of relevant comparisons of company taxation and company income at equivalent points in trade cycles. The following points should be borne in mind:-

(i) The table exaggerates total taxation because for ease of comparison tax on distributions made by companies has been included. (With help from the departments it should be possible for the Royal Commission to arrive at equivalent estimates *excluding* tax on distributions.)

(ii) Investment grants have been deducted from the tax totals in the National Expenditure blue book.

(iii) The figure for "accruals" taxation for 1973 is *prior* to the tax relief in the November budget. A crude approximation would be that for the last three-quarters of calendar 1973 this relief would reduce taxation on an accruals basis by £580 million. Because of uncertainty as to the actual effect of the tax relief in terms of national accounts procedures this has not been included in the table, but an approximate estimate of its effect is added in the text following the table itself.

(iv) The total of company "gross trading profit" is subject to the criticism (that it is substantially and increasingly less than the gross trading profits of industrial and commercial companies) outlined above.

Unfortunately the National Income and Expenditure accounts do not allow even the inadequately detailed analysis of taxation and income available for the company sector as a whole to be applied to the aggregates of "industrial and commercial companies".

The table on page 30 indicates a distinct fall in the proportional rate of tax *payments* for 1973 as compared with the earlier years chosen. On an "accruals" basis there appears little change in relation to either "gross trading profits" or "company income arising in the UK less interest payments outside the company sector" for 1973 compared with earlier years. But if three quarters of the £775 million tax relief already mentioned can be attributed to calendar 1973, then the proportion of taxation on an accruals basis comes down to 22% of "company income arising in the UK", to 33% of "gross trading profits", and to only 30% of "company income arising in the UK less interest payments outside the company sector". This is quite a dramatic fall in tax incidence compared with the earlier years chosen for comparison. It clearly represents a very substantial concession to the emphasis placed on provision for stock appreciation in recent discussions.

**TABLE I**
**TAXATION AND COMPANY INCOME**
*(£ million)*

| | *1960* | *1964* | *1973* |
|---|---|---|---|
| **Taxation** | | | |
| Accruals | 1,550 | 1,747 | 3,409 |
| Payments | 1,216 | 1,473 | 2,352 |
| **Company Income** | | | |
| Arising in UK | 4,578 | 5,595 | 12,611 |
| Gross Trading Profits | 3,736 | 4,544 | 8,476 |
| Arising in UK *less* interest paid | 4,147 | 4,942 | 9,378 |
| **Taxation on "accruals" basis as a percentage of:-** | | | |
| **Company Income** | | | |
| Arising in UK | 34 | 31 | 27 |
| Gross trading profits | 42 | 39 | 40 |
| Arising in UK *less* interest paid | 37 | 35 | 36 |
| **Taxation payments as a percentage of:-** | | | |
| **Company Income** | | | |
| Arising in UK | 27 | 26 | 19 |
| Gross trading profits | 33 | 33 | 28 |
| Arising in UK *less* interest paid | 29 | 30 | 25 |

Moreover, the reduction in the weight of company taxation is in sharp contrast with the *increased severity* of taxation in relation to wage and salary incomes. Thus in 1960 *income tax* on wages and salaries accounted for *just under 8%* of the total paybill (wages and salaries); by 1973 the weight of income tax was *14%* of total wages and salaries. Over the same period *net indirect taxation* as a proportional addition to "factor cost" consumer expenditure rose from *just under 15% to a little over 18%.* Simply putting these elements of direct and indirect taxation together suggests that approximately central government taxation falling on wages and salaries rose from around 23% of pre-tax income to 32%. (This does not take into account the increased severity of incidence of employees' national insurance contributions and payments of local rates.)

The previous sections of this paper have made clear the care that needs to be taken in assessing alleged declines in profitability in the UK economy in recent years. Thus on one measure, for large quoted companies in manufacturing, distribution, and other services, post-tax net income after all interest charges, expressed as a proportion of shareholders' interest, had by 1972 risen to a level not previously experienced in equivalent years in previous trade cycles (indeed, higher than the *peak* year of previous trade cycles):-

| | |
|---|---|
| 1959 | 10.3% |
| 1963 | 8.5% |
| 1968 | 8.8% |
| 1972 | 13.1% |

(*Economic Trends*, November 1974, p. xli)

In the same table in the *Economic Trends* article a different approach results in apparently steeply falling series for trends in profit ratios. This arises from putting together those elements in inflation accounting that produce a pessimistic view of profitability, and considering such profit series only pre-tax. As has been indicated above, the 1973 outturn must look substantially different post-tax.

It seems pertinent here to draw attention to the study by M.A. King reported in the NIESR *Economic Review* for November 1974 and to the further estimates that the NIESR make there in updating King's figures.

For manufacturing industry King measured gross trading profits in relation to total value added in the sector. He found that for the period 1950-73 the apparent underlying downward trend in gross trading profits as a share of value added was essentially a "pre-tax" phenomenon; post tax "there is no evidence of a similar secular decline". The deduction of stock appreciation from profits did produce a falling trend, but significantly an application of inflation accounting on a CPP (constant purchasing power) basis showed for 1973 a major recovery in manufacturing profitability post tax and post depreciation and stock appreciation provision. The ratio of profits to value added on this basis is shown as rising from 13% in 1972 to over 16% in 1973. (Unfortunately the Table, on p. 22 of the NIESR *Economic Review* for November 1974, does not make clear whether this calculation was made *before* the additional tax relief provided by the November 1974 budget or *after*.) At least it is clear that this contrasts with the more partial studies, such as those tabulated in the November 1974 *Economic Trends* article.

*Trends 1964-1973*

At the risk of being accused of misinterpretation of data (and in the light of all that has been argued so far in this paper the risk is clearly there), it does seem worthwhile to summarise *some* of the main relationships that emerge from *National Income and Expenditure, 1963-1973.* The years used for purposes of comparison are in the first place 1964 and 1973 as being as near as possible equivalent years (peak years) in the trade cycle. The emergence of declining profitability trends from the mid-1960s ("Company profitability has been steadily declining since the mid 1960s": R. Bateman, CBI, 2 October 1974) has been argued quite widely, so that the comparison across approximately the last decade seems particularly suitable. (*Within* the decade there is a sharp contrast also between the pressure on profits up to 1970 and the extensive improvement from 1970 to 1973.)

It has already been suggested that if what is examined is the relationship between the growth of company income on the one hand and the national product on the other, then some care has to be taken as to which series is most appropriately compared with which.

a) To compare aggregates before providing for depreciation and stock appreciation, the measure of the national product that seems most useful is that of "total domestic incomes". At current prices and taking 1964 as 100 this rose to an index figure of 220 in 1973 (£64.7 billion).

b) Company sector income arising in the UK rose slightly faster; taking 1964 as 100 it stood at 225 in 1973 (£12.6 bn.). It might be thought more appropriate to measure this aggregate *after* interest payments to recipients outside the company sector; on this basis the 1973 index (1964 as 100) was 190 (£9.4 billion). On this latter basis, company income as a proportion of total domestic incomes fell from 16.8% in 1964 to 14.5% in 1973. However, this is "pre-tax". Actual tax paid (including tax on distributed income) fell as a proportion of company income (it has been shown that so did tax on an "accruals" basis, taking into account the November 1974 budget relief, but this presents problems of estimation). Company income *after* interest payments to other sectors and *after* actual tax payments in the year increased (1964 as 100) to an index of 203 in 1973; as a proportion of total domestic incomes the fall in share was only from 11.8% to 10.8%.

c) The only reasonably reliable series from which to record changes in gross trading profits would seem to be that for *non-nationalised* industrial and commercial companies. (The nationalisation of major steel companies serves to deflate somewhat the series for industrial and commercial companies after 1967 as compared with pre 1967; hence the non-nationalised companies present a clearer picture.) Over the period from 1964 to 1973 non-nationalised industrial and commercial companies almost exactly doubled their gross trading profits (taking 1964 as 100 the index for 1973 is 197; £9.24 billion in 1973). Unfortunately it is not possible from the national accounts as so far presented to disentangle the tax payments in each year on a strictly equivalent basis. But there need be no doubt that the tendency of the tax incidence would be to raise the 1973 index for post-tax profits compared with 1964.

d) Replacement cost "capital consumption" – estimates for which are of course subject to a considerable margin of error – is estimated to have risen (1964 as 100) to an index number of 244 for the industrial and commercial company sector by 1973 (to £2.6 billion). This is not substantially faster than the approximate doubling of gross trading profits. After taking replacement cost depreciation into account, trading profits of the industrial and commercial companies show a limited decline between 1964 and 1973 as a proportion of "total domestic incomes" *net* of capital consumption from approximately 14% in 1964 to 11½% in 1973. But it again has to be emphasised that this is a pretax comparison, and over the period depreciation allowances became more generous. (Thus by 1973 depreciation allowances for companies had risen to two and a half times their 1964 level, not taking into account the disbursement of over £200 million of investment grants in 1973.)

# 2

# The ownership of Shares

## Introduction

The advantages accruing from the ownership of equity shares raise the key consideration of whether a rigid distinction can and should be made between income and wealth. This question is relevant not only to treatment for taxation purposes, but also to any analysis of the distribution of income and wealth. We are convinced that the only correct approach – in accordance with both economic rationality and overall equity – has to be that adopted by the Memorandum of Dissent in the *Report of the Royal Commission on Taxation* (Cmnd 9474, 1955, pp. 355-6), which may be summarised thus:

> "In our view the taxable capacity of an individual consists in his power to satisfy his own material needs, i.e. to attain a particular living standard. We know of no alternative definition that is capable of satisfying society's prevailing sense of fairness and equity. Thus the ruling test to be applied in deciding whether any particular receipt should or should not be reckoned as taxable income is whether it contributes or not, or how far it contributes, to an individual's 'spending power' during a period . . .
>
> In fact no concept of income can really be equitable that stops short of the comprehensive definition which embraces all receipts which increase an individual's command over the use of society's scarce resources – in other words, his 'net accretion of economic power between two points of time'."

The above definition focuses attention on two fundamental aspects of the concept of income which reflects the increment of 'spending power' or 'economic power' in a period. One is that income is a measure of the increase in the individual's command over resources in a period, irrespective of how much or how little of that command he actually exercises in consumption. The private choice of an individual as to how much he spends and how much he saves is irrelevant to this notion: income is the sum of consumption and net saving. The second is that 'net saving' (and hence income) includes the whole of the change in the value of man's store of property rights between two points of time, irrespective of whether the change has been brought about by the current addition to property which is saving in the narrower sense, or whether it has been caused by accretions to the value of property. From the point of view of an individual's command over resources, it is the change in the real value of his property which alone matters, and not the process by which that change was brought about.

These contentions, generally acknowledged by economists (see A.B. Atkinson, *Unequal Shares,* Allen Lane, 1972, pp. 31-32), are particularly relevant to any consideration of the distribution of equity share ownership and of the income arising therefrom, for the owner of an ordinary share has title to two main potential benefits (we say "main" since he may also have privileged access to rights and/or bonus issues – an increasing tendency dealt with elsewhere in our evidence);

a) he is entitled to receive a dividend as recommended by the Directors of the Company; and

b) he commands a marketable asset the value of which will reflect any build-up of retained or undistributed profits "earned for equity".

It is important to note here at the outset that the current low market values of shares reflected by the stock market merely indicate a loss of confidence on the part of investors, and in no way a real or permanent writing-down of the capitalisation value of companies and their assets. The recent levels of the *Financial Times* Index have to be seen in the context of a cyclical pattern of investment activity and attitudes as well as against the particular current circumstances of the domestic and world economies.

### *The Pattern of Ownership of Equity Shares*

There are two reasons for concentrating on the ownership pattern rather than the distribution of dividend income. First, as indicated above, the income of companies accruing to shareholders in excess of distributed dividends is broadly represented by undistributed income. The latest figures (*National Income and Expenditure,* 1974, HMSO, page 34) show that undistributed income after taxation, at £6,396 million was nearly four times the value of dividends on ordinary shares (excluding imputed corporation tax) at £1,675 million. In such circumstances it would clearly be misleading to imply that the only – let alone the main – advantage accruing to shareholders is in the form of distributed dividends.

The second reason for considering the pattern of share ownership is more practical, in that rather more data is available. Inland Revenue Statistics do not distinguish within investment or unearned income between dividends and interest of various kinds, an omission to which the Royal Commission may well wish to recommend rectification.

There appear to be two sets of inequality of distribution of share ownership, direct and indirect. The former reflects the marked concentration of personal holdings of shares in the hands of comparatively few wealthy individuals, whilst the latter represents a rather more subtle set of inequalities within the institutional categories of shareholders. Each of these is considered below in turn.

*Personal Holdings of Shares*

The main official source of data here are the Inland Revenue Statistics. The degree of concentration of share ownership is really quite remarkable, particularly when it is remembered that the figures relate only to holders of dutiable wealth (some 44.2% of the population over 15). The following picture emerges from Table 94 of the 1973 Edition (pages 136–8):

TABLE 2

RANGE OF NET CAPITAL VALUE OF ESTATE

| | *Over £10,000* | *Under £10,000* |
|---|---|---|
| **Type of asset** | **% of total value held:** | |
| Shares and Debentures in Companies: | | |
| British unquoted: ordinary | 94.5 | 5.5 |
| preference, debentures | 96.5 | 4.5 |
| British quoted: ordinary: | | |
| investment trusts | 95.7 | 4.3 |
| others | 94.8 | 5.2 |
| preference, debentures | 90.5 | 9.5 |
| Overseas | 96.9 | 3.1 |
| Unit trusts | 70.8 | 29.2 |
| All securities and shares (including Government and Municipal securities) | 92.7 | 7.3 |

It is worth noting that those with estates valued at over £10,000 represented only 12% of wealth holders, and thus only 5.3% of the total population over 15.

This kind of picture has been confirmed for previous years by other researchers, who have also demonstrated that the concentration is even more marked when more sensitive gradations for wealth ranges are taken, and that the concentration is exceptionally acute for company stocks and shares compared with other forms of wealth, even though total personal wealth is highly concentrated overall. Illustrations of these tendencies, referred to by Atkinson (op. cit. p. 30-1) are produced below.

**TABLE 3**
**WEALTH AND THE COMPOSITION OF PORTFOLIOS 1957-59**
**RANGE OF WEALTH (£)**

| *Percentage of wealth in form of:* | 3,000 – | 10,000 | 50,000 – | 250,000 |
|---|---|---|---|---|
| Cash and bank deposits | 20 | 13 | 9 | 8 |
| Building Society deposits | 10 | 10 | 6 | 1 |
| Insurance Policies | 10 | 7 | 3 | 5 |
| British government securities | 9 | 7 | 9 | 4 |
| Company securities | 3 | 24 | 44 | 38 |
| Land and buildings | 34 | 20 | 13 | 22 |

*Source:* Revell, J.R.S., 'Assets and Age', *Bulletin of the Oxford Institute of Economics and Statistics,* August 1962. Table II.

**TABLE 4**
**CONCENTRATION OF OWNERSHIP OF DIFFERENT ASSETS 1954**

| | *Percentage owned by top:* | | |
|---|---|---|---|
| | *1%* | *5%* | *10%* |
| Cash and bank deposits | 23 | 48 | 64 |
| Government securities | 42 | 71 | 83 |
| Land, buildings and trade assets | 28 | 58 | 74 |
| Company stocks and shares | 81 | 96 | 98 |
| Total personal wealth | 43 | 68 | 79 |

*Source:* Lydall, H.F. and Tipping D.G., 'The Distribution of Personal Wealth in Britain', *Bulletin of the Oxford University Institute of Economics and Statistics,* February 1961. Table V.

It is also interesting to note that there is no evidence, on the basis of a comparison between Lydall and Tipping's figures and our own above, of any reduction in the degree of concentration of share ownership over the period 1954-71. The figures show that in both years some 95% of company shares were owned by the wealthiest 5% of the population.

### *Institutional Shareholders*

It is often argued that there has been a strong trend over the post-war period towards an increase in institutional as opposed to personal shareholdings, and that this represents an equalising tendency. Neither of these contentions can be taken at face value, however.

The change in proportionate ownership of shares has been usefully summarised by John Moyle (*The Pattern of Ordinary Share Ownership 1957-70,* University of Cambridge D.A.E. Occasional Paper 31, CUP 1971 page 7) as follows:

TABLE 5
REGISTERED SHAREHOLDERS, 1957-1969

| *Category of holder* | *Percentages of total market value* | | |
|---|---|---|---|
| | *1957* | *1963* | *1970* |
| Persons, executors & trustees | 61.8 | 51.0 | 44.7 |
| Insurance | 8.0 | 9.2 | 10.6 |
| Banks & nominee companies | 13.5 | 20.2 | 21.2 |
| Pension funds | 1.2 | 2.9 | 4.9 |
| Investment trusts | 3.0 | 3.2 | 4.2 |
| Other finance | 1.6 | 2.6 | 1.2 |
| Charities & non-profit | 1.3 | 1.8 | 1.8 |
| Non-financial companies | 1.9 | 3.5 | 3.9 |
| Public sector | 3.9 | 1.7 | 3.8 |
| Overseas | 3.8 | 3.8 | 3.7 |
| Total | 100.0 | 100.0 | 100.0 |

Whilst there is no doubt that personal holdings have significantly reduced as a proportion of the total, this has not been fully taken up by insurance and pension funds, or investment trusts (often held to be the main equalising institutions, but see below), but also by banks and nominee companies, and by non-financial companies. Whilst some of these beneficial holdings are held on behalf of the institutions, others reinforce personal and company share ownership. Moyle (op.cit. p.18) offers a comparable analysis by beneficial ownership:

TABLE 6
BENEFICIAL OWNERS, 1957-1969

| *Category of holder* | *Percentages of market value* | | |
|---|---|---|---|
| | *1957* | *1963* | *1970* |
| Persons, executors & trustees | 65.8 | 54.0 | 47.4 |
| Insurance | 8.8 | 10.0 | 12.2 |
| Pension funds | 3.4 | 6.4 | 9.0 |
| Investment trusts | 5.2 | 7.4 | 7.6 |
| Unit trusts | .5 | 1.3 | 2.9 |
| Banks | .9 | 1.3 | 1.7 |
| Stock exchange | .9 | 1.4 | 1.4 |
| Other finance | 1.6 | 2.6 | 1.1 |
| Non-profit | 1.9 | 2.1 | 2.1 |
| Non-financial companies | 2.7 | 5.1 | 5.4 |
| Public sector | 3.9 | 1.5 | 2.6 |
| Overseas | 4.4 | 7.0 | 6.6 |
| Total | 100.00 | 100.0 | 100.0 |

It can be seen that whilst the rates of increase in ownership by institutions are quite rapid, they only account for some two-thirds of the decline in personal holdings; the rest is taken up by banks, stock exchange, non-financial companies and overseas.

Also worth noting from Moyle's figures is that whilst persons account for 44.7% of registered holdings, they represent 47.4% of beneficial ownership.

We are sceptical of the argument that the growth of institutional shareholdings represents an unqualified trend towards greater equality of share ownership. There can be no doubt that the advertising material of investment and unit trusts recognises established wealth-holders and high-income recipients as its potential targets; life assurance and pension fund contributions, savings and investments are not significant features until high income-levels are reached; and there are still sharp divisions between different categories of workers so far as coverage and value of company pension arrangements are concerned.

One source of data here is the *Family Expenditure Survey* (HMSO 1973, Tables 1 and 36), from which the following latest figures are derived:

TABLE 7

| *Weekly income of household* | *Income derived from investments* | *Payments on: life assurance & contributions to pension funds* | *savings and investments* |
|---|---|---|---|
| £ | £.p. | £.p. | £.p. |
| Under 10 | 0.17 | 0.11 | 0.08 |
| 10 – 25 | 0.36 | 0.16 | 0.10 |
| 15 – 20 | 0.89 | 0.24 | 1.40* |
| 20 – 25 | 1.05 | 0.40 | 0.12 |
| 25 – 30 | 0.84 | 0.67 | 0.19 |
| 30 – 35 | 0.82 | 0.94 | 0.22 |
| 35 – 40 | 0.85 | 1.15 | 0.32 |
| 40 – 45 | 0.90 | 1.90 | 0.60 |
| 45 – 50 | 1.22 | 1.32 | 0.66 |
| 50 – 60 | 1.13 | 1.86 | 0.74 |
| 60 – 70 | 1.42 | 2.31 | 1.11 |
| 70 – 80 | 1.64 | 2.96 | 1.07 |
| 80 – 100 | 2.68 | 3.67 | 2.08 |
| 100 or more | 10.39 | 6.64 | 5.83* |

(*figure has relatively high sampling error)

Data on coverage and value of private pension and superannuation arrangements can be put together from various sources, all of which point to inequalities of both access and benefit. Thus the Department of Employment's 1968 survey of labour costs (*Employment and Productivity Gazette*, August and October 1970, January 1971) indicated the following for all manufacturing industries:

TABLE 8

| | *All employees* | *Operatives* | *Administrative, Technical and Clerical Employees* |
|---|---|---|---|
| **Superannuation & Private Pension Funds** | | | |
| % of employers making contribution | 71.7 | 49.5 | 71.7 |
| Average expenditure per employee: annually | 32.6 | 14.4 | 79.1 |
| **Group Life Insurance** | | | |
| % of employers making contribution | 36.9 | 26.5 | 36.9 |
| Average expenditure per employee: £ annually | 2.7 | 1.2 | 6.4 |

Without exception it is clear that manual workers are at substantial disadvantages with regard to both coverage and value. A more recent study by Incomes Data Services (*Occupational Pensions – Part 2*, Study No. 71, March 1974, page 3) drew attention to the Fourth Survey by the Government Actuary in 1971, which showed:

"Manual workers are more likely to be excluded from company schemes than are staff. They are also less likely to have their pensions increased against the cost of living, after retirement. Contributions and thus benefits, are often lower. In 60% of the manual schemes surveyed, employee contributions were less than 3% of salary, and in 82% of schemes, contributions were less than 4%. In staff schemes however, levels were generally higher, with 58% of schemes requiring 5% – 6% contributions and 11% of schemes requires 6% and over.

The most significant distinctions appear in the type of schemes used. Manual workers were far less likely, in 1971, to be members of final salary schemes, and even where final salary benefits were provided, they were based on a lower fraction of pay.

TABLE 10
PRIVATE SECTOR

| | *Staff members* | *Manual members* |
|---|---|---|
| **Pension Scheme** | | |
| Final salary | 76% | 24% |
| Average salary | 12% | 9% |
| Flat rate accrual | 4% | 57% |
| **Pension fractions** | | |
| Less than 80ths | 3% | 74% |
| 80ths | 22% | 7% |
| 80ths – 60ths | 8% | 15% |
| 60ths or better | 67% | 4% |

The discrepancies in pension arrangements as between men and women as well as between manual and non-manual workers were also described in "Private Pensions or State Benefits", T.E. Chester (*National Westminster Bank Quarterly Review,* August 1972):

> "about two-thirds of all male employees, roughly ten million, are covered by occupational pensions, but only about a quarter of female employees, some two million . . . only about 4.5 per cent of all women in part-time employment were enrolled in occupational schemes in 1970.
>
> All official surveys have shown, and recent data collected by the Department of Employment confirm, that white-collar workers may be enrolled to the extent of approximately 80 per cent, whereas the ratio for blue-collar workers will rarely be higher than 50 per cent. . . . The distinction between 'white' and 'blue' collar workers becomes even more significant when statistical returns show that those in the higher earning brackets can expect pension coverage reaching 90 per cent whereas that of an unskilled labourer with a low wage packet may be less than 25 per cent."

All this evidence is of significance to this paper in two senses. *First, it is clear that the tendency towards increased institutional shareholding by pension funds cannot be held to represent an equalising force when discrepancies between different categories of employee are so striking.* A secondary pattern of inequality and concentration is merely being gradually grafted onto the primary unequal distribution of individual share ownership.

*Second, it is equally apparent that where company income is allocated towards private social welfare payments on behalf of employees, the main beneficiaries are not manual workers.* Indeed, further concentration within the "administrative, technical and clerical" category becomes evident from company reports and accounts which acknowledge massive pension provision for directors, ex-directors and senior executives. Courtaulds, for example, allocated £196,000 under this heading in 1974. More analysis of directors' and executives' pay and benefits is being submitted by the TGWU in its evidence to the general reference of the Royal Commission on the Distribution of Income and Wealth, but it is important also here in this context to draw attention to the substantial fringe benefits accorded out of company income to directors and senior executives.

We must emphasise that we are not here rejecting the *potential* of private pension funds as a force towards social ownership. But as long as pension and superannuation arrangements aggravate existing income and other inequalities, and remain largely out of control and accountability as far as employees and their trade unions are concerned, they cannot fulfil this kind of role. Moreover, since pension funds have largely concentrated their holdings in the larger companies and have spread their holdings to spread risks, they have not generally been particularly active influences upon company management. Consequently, they have had less influence than might be supposed on the *control* of industry, which has remained more in the hands of boards of directors, or of family and other groups retaining large shareholdings for control purposes.

In summary, the development of private pension funds and their role as major institutional shareholders cannot be regarded as a realistic and unqualified tendency towards social ownership and equality unless and until the following conditions, which are not at present satisfied, are met:

(i) they must be more widely accessible to all categories of workers;
(ii) they must not amplify and reinforce existing inequalities;
(iii) the management of their funds must be made more accountable to employees; and
(iv) they must begin to exert a more active control function over companies whose shares they hold.

# 3

# The Nature of Equity Shareholding

It is often argued that equity shareholders have a justifiable claim upon company income – particularly in terms of any build up of the capital value of shares – since they provide risk capital. It is further currently argued that the present low market price levels of equities are firm evidence of the real risks involved for investors in companies. In this paper we set out to place these arguments in perspective and to stress certain qualifications to them.

We are not of course denying that a crisis of financial confidence exists: this is evident from the overwhelming preference for cash amongst investors. But we feel it is important to distinguish qualitatively different elements of risk involved, and to indicate those tendencies which over a longer term have diluted risk.

First, equity prices must necessarily be seen against the background of a strongly marked trade cycle, which means that comparisons between points in time must take this into account. Second, risks have been most acute in the property and financial sector rather than in industrial and commercial companies, particularly in cases where over-borrowing from an insecure asset base was involved. Third, the predominance of multi-product and often multi-national companies in the British economy is a stabilising force. And fourth, the spreading of risks across these major industrial companies in portfolios by major institutional and private shareholders offers further protection against risk elements. For all these reasons it is necessary to distinguish speculative risk elements from the mainstream performance of major equities.

In this context it is relevant to note that private pension funds during 1974 increased their net investment in UK equities by £88m from a level at the end of 1973 of £2,948 market value, which represented 48% of their total holdings. (*Pension Fund Performance*, Phillips and Drew.)

We now turn to those longer-term developments which have influenced the nature of equity share-holding, and which qualify its traditional role.

*Sources of funds*

Share issues have come to represent an almost negligible fraction of the sources of company funds. In only one of the last eight years have equity issues provided more than 5% of total funds, whilst in 1970 and 1973 the proportion fell below 1%. Figures derived from the CSO's Financial Statistics show the percentage of capital funds of industrial and commercial companies in the UK provided by capital issues of quoted companies as follows:

| *Year* | *Ordinary Shares* | *Debentures & Preference shares (net)* |
|---|---|---|
| 1966 | 3.2 | 11.8 |
| 7 | 1.6 | 8.6 |
| 8 | 5.5 | 3.3 |
| 9 | 3.1 | 5.8 |
| 70 | 0.7 | 2.6 |
| 1 | 2.4 | 3.4 |
| 2 | 3.3 | 3.0 |
| 3 | 0.7 | 0.4 |

Alongside this negligible role as providers of new capital for companies, the equity shareholder retains the right to potential benefit from undistributed company income through the build-up of *future* capacity and *future* income for equity. Moreover, it can be argued that this potential build-up of benefit on behalf of the equity shareholder is understated by the measure of retained profits (see R.M. Titmuss, *Income Distribution and Social Change,* Allen and Unwin, 1962, page 109 and following). Whilst the problems of inflation accounting (discussed below) throw uncertainties upon the measurement of this potential build-up, its long-run presence cannot be doubted. One estimate, by stockbrokers de Zoete and Bevan, for the period 1919–1968 showed an average annual appreciation in the capital value of equity shares of 30 leading industrial companies of 4.7%, or 2.7% in real terms. (Atkinson, *op.cit.* p. 35.)

The moral is that the legal rights of the equity shareholders contrast sharply with the very limited extent to which the finance of company sector development in recent years has rested on *additional* provision of equity capital. Equity Capital issues have been only of marginal importance in helping finance *real* capital formation (their main role has been in providing the "paper" for waves of company take-over activity). Thus, there is a striking difference between the marginal contribution made to corporate capital raising on the part of equity capital, and the legal claim to control the use and disposal of the real resources of the company sector.

And yet the risks of industry are clearly not those of the shareholders only; as a trade union we can testify that they are tangibly felt by workers and their communities. Nevertheless the long-run *rewards* and *claims* arising from and upon company income accrue to the equity shareholders alone.

*Acquisitions and Takeovers*

These considerations are particularly pertinent when closer attention is paid to the contemporary role of equity shares in stock market transactions as well as new issues, for their main role has been the financing of company take-over activity. CSO Financial Statistics data show that half of total expenditure on acquisitions and mergers in recent years is in the form of ordinary shares; the peak expenditure in this form, in 1972, totalled £1,459 million, representing 58% of the total. (These figures relate to industrial and commercial companies; for financial companies the proportionate role of ordinary shares in financing take-over activity has been greater still).

It is in the circumstances of take-over activity inspired more often by financial strategy than by economic rationality or social responsibility, that workers have felt the full brunt of the risks which they carry.

It is also in this area of activity that disclosure requirements (by both Government and Stock Exchange) and accountability principles (by the public agencies involved) leave so much to be desired. The key informational needs in connection with company income are discussed separately.

Moreover, take-over and merger activity is essentially designed to remove or minimise risk elements from corporate strategy and in consequence from equity shareholdings. The degree of concentration of ownership and control in British industry resulting from the massive increase in mergers and take-overs over the post-war period has served to reduce shareholders' risks and enhance their income and capital, often at the expense of the job security of the employees involved.

*Pricing and Inflation Accounting*

The greater the degree of concentration of managerial control in industry, the wider the scope for administered pricing policies immune from conventional market pressures. Until the introduction of tighter price controls, this freedom represented the key ability for companies to enhance the value of equity shareholdings by boosting undistributed company income. One of the key arguments for the retention and development of the price control administrative system is the obligations and disciplines placed upon private sector management by the Price Code and the requirements of the Prices Commission notification system, despite the premium of confidentiality placed upon this sphere of our nation's economic life.

It has been argued more recently (especially by the CBI and the Institute of Chartered Accountants) that company earnings are really exaggerated by the going rate of inflation, and that adjustments to conventional company accounts are required if a true picture is to be presented. Whilst the existence of an inflation impact on depreciation and stock appreciation items derived from orthodox accounting procedures is undeniable, we have several reservations about the use of any adjustment mechanism based upon a general index (such as the 'current purchasing power' approach recommended by the Institute of Chartered Accountants). Our reservations here are in line with the evidence submitted by the Trade Union Research Unit to the Inflation Accounting Committee (1974)*, and the article in *Economic Trends:* 'Accounting for Inflation', A.H. Cowley, August 1974. We are not only conscious of the wide scope for enhancement of corporate control and minimisation of corporate tax liability if the ICA's recommendations were to be effected; we are also aware of the extent to which the equity interest in a company can be protected – and indeed advanced – as a result of capital gearing and company borrowing policies. At some stage a distinction will have to be made within any inflation accounting recommendations between the company's performance and its shareholders' interest.

*Financial Relations with Government*

Our final point on the real nature of equity shareholding reflects the growing financial interdependence between the private company and the State. There are three themes here which reduce either the risk element or the financial obligations of companies, or both.

(i) The increased role and value of investment grants represents a substantial offset. Over the past five years investment grants have far exceeded the contribution of ordinary share issues in relation to sources of capital funds for industry (CSO Financial Statistics). Tony Benn, Secretary of State for Industry, has revealed that between 1970 and 1974 £3,075 million has been paid out by the State under the various subsidy programmes, which compares with £6,375 million paid in tax by companies, or share dividends of £6,508 million paid out by companies, in the same period.

(ii) This leads into the area of corporate taxation and tax allowances, where several trends and changes in the post-war British requirements have operated in favour of company income and the or-

---

*See Appendix p.56 ff.

dinary shareholder. A combination of reduced rates of corporation tax (until recently) and enhanced tax allowances (particularly for depreciation) has served to reduce overall tax liability for the corporate sector. We deal with this question more fully elsewhere in our evidence.

At the same time the switch from April 1973 to the imputation system of corporation tax represents an ill-advised incentive for companies to replace emphasis upon distributed profits, notwithstanding dividend controls. In current circumstances, and in the light of recent past performance, there is no evidence that new capital will be voluntarily directed into productive industry in response to this fiscal incentive. There is no reason to believe that high distribution would help to maintain the real level of capital formation: if anything the evidence is quite the contrary. Moreover we see no reason why the level of taxation falling on distributed dividends should be reduced, which is an intended effect of the imputation system of corporation tax.

Our concern about a tax system which may encourage high rates of dividend distribution (at least in the absence of statutory restraint on increases in dividends) is clearly particularly relevant at the present time. It would hardly help the rate of real capital formation in 1975 if companies were to be generally increasing dividend distribution and then having to cover additional investment financing requirements by borrowing e.g. from FFI at an interest rate of around 16%. At present there is an obvious tension between the philosophy of the "imputation" system of corporation tax, which ended the encouragement the 1965 Corporation Tax system gave to relatively high retention rates*, and the official constraints on dividend distribution. We do not think this tension should be overcome by freeing dividends from restraint. Rather, the economic logic of the nation's need for a stronger real investment programme points to a resolution of the tension by a return to the 1965 Corporation Tax system. Nothing that has happened recently suggests that there was any error in the reasoning of the famous Minority Report of the Royal Commission on Taxation which led to the form of Corporation Tax introduced in 1965.

---

* In simple terms if dividend cover was more than 1.8 the new "imputation" system increased the weight of company taxation as compared with the previous Corporation Tax system; if dividend cover were under 1.8 then the proportion taken in tax fell.

# 4

# The Privileged Tax Position of Wealthy Shareholders

Since the change-over to the "imputation" system of corporation tax an increasing number of UK companies are offering their ordinary shareholders a choice of receiving their dividends in the normal way as cash, or in the form of additional ordinary shares. (Previously, under section 236 of the 1970 Finance Act companies were required to pay income tax on the "scrip" dividend, and the shareholder had to pay surtax – if liable – on the gross amount of the dividend.)

The new approach actually represents an extremely inequitable easing of the taxation system solely to benefit higher rate taxpayers. As a consequence it represents a serious erosion of the tax base. Since dividends on ordinary shares must by 1975 be over £1,800 million a year, the loss of tax revenue can be expected to be very high. A simple account of how the new scrip dividends schemes work will make the situation clear.

Since the basic tax rate on dividend distribution is paid at source by the company (the so called "tax credit") the shareholder who is only taxed at the standard rate will have no further tax to pay. But, of course, most sizeable shareholdings held by private individuals will not be in that standard rate category. As soon as the taxpayer's income (after personal allowances) from all sources exceeds £4,500 he is liable to pay more than the standard rate: there will also be a surcharge on his investment income once it exceeds £1,000 p.a. The additional tax that a shareholder with higher income has to pay can vary between 5% and 50%, additionally there may be the investment income surcharge (up to 15%). Roughly speaking, the new scrip dividend system is designed to offer a flexible method of avoiding these higher tax rates which is likely to be generally advantageous to any shareholder whose additional tax rate is around 25% or more.

The normal form of the schemes is as follows. When a company announces its dividend it proposes also that shareholders who wish to can take the option of scrip in lieu of dividend. No dealing or stamp costs are involved for the shareholder who exercises the option. The value of the scrip is calculated by reference to the average price of the ordinary shares at some period prior to the announcement and approximates to the value of the net dividend. In essence the shareholder choosing to take the scrip dividend secures a *capital gain* which will be subject to a maximum 30% tax rate in place of an *income* which will be subject to progressive taxation.

(Example: assume gross dividend of £100, net dividend of £67, tax credit 33%, or alternative of shares to value of £67. If the shares are realised, maximum tax rate is 30%, i.e. approx. £20. This is therefore only less attractive than the cash dividend if the additional income tax payable on the cash dividend is no more than 20%. A shareholder with 40% additional tax to pay could save approximately £20 by opting for the scrip issue; a shareholder with an additional 60% to pay could save £40. To put it another way the maximum tax rate payable comes down to *little over 50%*, i.e. the "tax credit" foregone and 30% tax on the remainder.)

In practice the situation is rather more uncertain, but this uncertainty may *increase* the benefit secured by the shareholder. For the market value of the shares may rise between the date of the market quotations used by the company in determining how many new ordinary shares will be issued as scrip in relation to the stock already held and the date when the "election" to take a scrip issue is made; the price may rise further still by the time the stock is issued. Thus, on a falling market shareholders may choose to take their cash dividend rather than assume the element of risk as to realisation of their capital gain if they take the scrip option. But on a rising market for the company's ordinary shares the offer of scrip would look even more attractive. Besides, the shareholder taking the scrip option has far more flexibility as to when he chooses to realise his gain, and therefore may not only pay less tax but defer his tax liability till a later date.

As the approach is rapidly becoming standard company practice the losses involved for the government revenue must mount. Supposing no more than 40% of total dividends to be received by individuals who would have had to pay on average 35% in tax over and above their tax credit, the immediate loss to the exchequer would be around £250 million a year if these individuals opted for the scrip (but did not immediately realise their scrip). Even if half the scrip were realised in the same year and attracted a 30% tax rate the revenue loss would still be around £180 million.

This is socially intolerable and inequitable, not least in a period in which the income tax structure is hitting more severely workers on below average incomes.

It need hardly be said that there is no advantage to the exchequer and the wider community in all this. Indeed, it should be emphasised that part of the loss to the revenue arises from another feature of the "imputation" system. This is that when companies pay out cash dividends they are called on to pay Advance Corporation Tax (and for the present year an additional surcharge). When they issue full paid scrip shares they are not liable to ACT and consequently are able to conserve cash – both the cash that would have been paid out in net dividend (instead of which they merely issue their own paper) and the cash that would have been paid over to the government (but which is now deferred to the date when eventually they have to pay their normal corporation tax). Not that the benefit to the company should be over-exaggerated: as has already been pointed out, in a period of falling prices (as recently) when companies might most wish to conserve cash there may be fewer takers for the scrip issue than in a period of optimism and rising share prices – when companies may be less concerned. Nevertheless, the system clearly does provide an incentive to companies to adopt the scrip issue approach as a way of conserving cash – but the *main* beneficiaries are quite simply the wealthy shareholders who have been offered a new means of avoiding progressive taxation.

The whole arrangement is socially pernicious and must be terminated. It is particularly ironic that it was initiated at a time when statutory incomes policies were holding down the incomes of employees in the name of, allegedly, "felt fairness". The scrip dividend system is an exercise in evident unfairness.

The most recent developments in the Stock Market (January 1975) and further indications that many more companies are offering scrip as an alternative to cash dividends have made the argument advanced here even more urgent.

It is clear that the combined attraction of improved cash flow and cash retention to the company and steep reduction in tax liability to the wealthier shareholders is rapidly making the offer of a scrip alternative general practice. In some cases this is being done in such unseemly haste that shareholders are being presented with a final date for "election" to receive an allotment of shares, in lieu of cash dividend, that is earlier than the date of the "extraordinary" general meeting called to pass the necessary resolutions to enable the proposals to come into effect. (English China Clays Limited is a case in point. It may be noted that in this company the Chairman, Lord Aberconway, is the beneficial owner of 1,644,273 shares, so that he clearly has a substantial personal interest in adopting the scrip option).

Earlier in this section it was pointed out that

"on a rising market for the company's ordinary shares the offer of a scrip would look even more attractive".

The steep rise in the market price of ordinary shares has not merely borne this out but provides some quite extreme examples of the inequity of the scrip dividend system. This is not simply a "loophole" in the structure of progressive taxation; it is clearly the most serious erosion of the base of progressive taxation to have appeared in recent years.

A specific example can demonstrate this point. We assume an ordinary shareholder with a medium sized holding of 10,000 shares in *Tesco.*

Tesco have announced an interim dividend of 0.5389p payable on 10th March 1975; that is the figure "net" of the tax credit – the "gross" equivalent is 0.8043p. If the shareholder received this dividend in the normal way, the post-tax income arising will depend on his marginal tax rate. The following are examples of possible marginal tax rates, in each case assuming investment income is over £2,000 and liable to the 15% surcharge:-

| *Taxable Income Band* | *Tax Rate* |
|---|---|
| 8,000 – 10,000 | 73% |
| 10,000 – 12,000 | 78% |
| 15,000 – 20,000 | 88% |

Thus, with 10,000 shares in Tesco, the shareholders would stand to receive the following post-tax income from the interim dividend:-

| | |
|---|---|
| 73% tax rate . . . . | £21.71 |
| 78% tax rate . . . . | £17.69 |
| 88% tax rate . . . . | £9.65 |

Now, suppose the shareholder opts instead to take up the scrip dividend option. This was determined by the company taking as the basis of calculation the middle market quotation for the shares for the five business days preceding 24th December 1974, as these were the days before the share price was quoted "ex dividend". The share price used was 21.9611p. Using that price the company estimated the issue of new shares that would approximately equal the value of the *net* cash dividend. What emerged was a scrip dividend option of one new share for every 40.7517 shares held. Our hypothetical shareholder with 10,000 shares is therefore entitled to receive 245 shares (fractions are disregarded).

The shareholder in this case had until the 7th February 1975 to determine whether to take up the share option. In early February the share price had risen to about 35p; on the 5th February (the last date on which he might safely post his option form) the preceding day's share price had been 33p.

Of course, if the shareholder takes up his share option and merely uses it to increase his holding to 10,245 shares the value of the scrip dividend to him is indeterminate. It depends on the future of the Tesco share price.

But there is a simple way of assessing the value to him of the scrip option at the time when he has to make his decision to take it up. For the shareholder could *at that point* sell 245 shares from his existing holding (he will thus retain a total holding of 10,000). The option must be worth *at least* that much to him, since if he retains his shares instead of selling them this is a preferred response to the choices facing him.

Assuming a 33p selling price, the net proceeds (after allowing for selling costs) would be about £78.65. The shareholder might be liable to capital gains taxation on this sum (though in the current financial year he is very likely to be able to "realise" losses to set off against this. But in order to continue to estimate the *least value* of the scrip dividend to him let us assume that he does (subsequently) incur capital gains tax, at 30%. The post-tax income he has secured from the scrip dividend emerges as just over £55.

This can now be compared with the post-tax income he would have secured from the cash dividend:-

If his marginal tax rate is 73% his post-tax income (from the scrip as contrasted with the cash dividend) is *at least 2.5 times* as great.

If his marginal tax rate is 78% his post-tax income is *at least 3.1 times* as great.

If his marginal tax rate is 88% his post-tax income is *at least 5.7 times* as great.

It should be emphasised that Tesco is taken as a typical recent example, not an extreme one. Other companies have had proportionately steeper share price increases between the date when the share price was calculated for distribution purposes and the date when the option to take up the scrip had to be made.

# 5

# Provision of Information by Companies

In our view it is necessary for the Royal Commission to direct attention towards the adequacy of information provision by companies under its Company Income Reference. We are conscious of the general improvements and developments required in the field of company law reform; and we also have considerable experience of the inadequacy of information disclosed by companies in the context of collective bargaining and joint consultation.

It is not our intention in this paper to offer a fully comprehensive and detailed discussion of the requirements involved, but rather to indicate the priority areas for consideration with particular reference to income from companies.

### *Company Law Reform*

The Conservative Government White Paper, *Company Law Reform* (July 1973, Cmnd. 5391) and the Labour Party Green Paper, *The Community and the Company* (May 1974) have each shifted discussion of issues forward in several key areas of concern. The emphasis in the Conservative approach was on regulation of insider dealings, disclosure of nominee shareholdings; disclosure of directors' interests; and obliging companies to be more up-to-date in filing their accounts. We endorse all these requirements (as did the Labour Party's approach), each of which is highly relevant to the accurate determination of income arising from companies as well as being of more general concern. This kind of information is needed to identify, on a timely basis, the real benefits arising to individuals and companies from their activities, and to develop adequate principles of accountability. The Labour Party approach also acknowledged the need for wider information on transactions between companies, subsidiaries, associated companies and pension fund managers, and for regular provision (as in the USA) of a flow of funds statement. Again these recommendations are highly relevant to questions of company income, as is the additional requirement, which we would add, for adequate disclosure of direct and indirect benefits for directors and executives and senior employees.

*Accounting Procedures*

In our view it is not sufficient to require a statutory minimum degree of information from companies: there is additionally great scope for more standardisation of accounting procedures, and for companies to adopt best practices in provision of more detailed and helpful information. In this context it is interesting to note the list of "examples of matters for which different accounting bases are recognised", (*Disclosure of Accounting Policies,* Statement of Standard Accounting Practice No. 2, Nov. 1971, Institute of Chartered Accountants, page 4).

- depreciation of fixed assets
- treatment and amortisation of intangibles such as research and development expenditure, patents and trademarks
- stocks and work in progress
- long-term contracts
- deferred taxation
- hire-purchase or instalment transactions
- leasing and rental transactions
- conversion of foreign currencies
- repairs and renewals
- consolidation policies
- property development transactions
- warranties for products or services

*Further Subjects for Disclosure*

Our experience as a trade union involved in collective bargaining activity in major industries suggests that the adequacy of information provided by companies on a statutory basis leaves a lot to be desired. This is true from a trade union point of view; from the more general standpoint of social accountability; and also in the context of analysing the sources and allocation of company income under this Reference. We would draw particular attention to the following key areas, *all of which are covered inadequately by minimum statutory obligations of disclosure:*

| | | | |
|---|---|---|---|
| 1. | *Manpower* | – | employment and payment structures |
| | | – | labour productivity and turnover |
| 2. | *Production* | – | real output |
| | | – | value added |

| | | | |
|---|---|---|---|
| 3. | *Financial* | – | non-trading income |
| | | – | acquisitions and disposals |
| 4. | *Investment* | – | capital expenditure |
| | | – | forward sanctions |
| | | – | depreciation policy |
| 5. | *Balance of Payments* | – | imports and exports |
| | | – | income paid to and received from abroad (including breakdowns by product and by country). Additionally, company information disclosure requirements which appear adequate may cease to become so in the case of multi-national companies. Here the key additional areas are: |
| 6. | *Sales* | – | breakdown by product and country |
| | | – | intra-company sales |
| 7. | *Profits* | – | depreciation procedures. |

# Appendix

# Inflation and Company Accounts

This Note was produced partly at the request of USDAW and partly in response to an invitation from the Inflation Accounting Committee, set up under Mr. Francis Sandilands by the Department of Trade and Industry in July 1973, for the Unit to submit evidence. The Note lists the main effects of inflation upon company finance, performance and accounts; describes the current purchasing power approach to inflation accounting proposed by the Institute of Chartered Accountants in England and Wales; and illustrates the scale and nature of actual adjustments which would be involved. The rest of the Note is given over to the TURU Evidence to the Inflation Accounting Committee, and the associated correspondence. While this note does not form part of the Evidence of the TGWU to the Royal Commission, it does bear a close relationship to that testimony.

*Introduction*

The question of adjustment of company accounts to reflect the impact of inflation has become increasingly important as the rate of inflation has accelerated. This Note has been produced in response to two developments in this context. First, the Unit has been requested by USDAW to give attention to the question of inflation accounting; and second the Unit was invited by the Inflation Accounting Committee, set up by the Department of Trade and Industry in July 1973, to present evidence. The second part of this Note consists of our Evidence, together with the correspondence between the Committee and the Unit. First however we deal more generally with the effects of inflation on company finance and accounts; we describe the nature of the form of inflation accounting ("current purchasing power accounting") advocated by the Institute of Chartered Accountants; and we illustrate the nature of the adjustments made to company accounts.

*The effects of inflation*

The main impact of inflation on company finance is felt through depreciation and the renewal of fixed assets, though it also has influence upon working capital (stocks and debtors), through borrowing, and on taxation.

(i) *Depreciation:*

Since the object of depreciation charges is to provide for the replacement of fixed assets, it follows that, during the period of inflation, the charges made on the basis of the historic cost of assets may under-provide for the actual replacement cost, with the further consequence that profits and retentions are overstated. However there are several possible offsetting factors here.

Depreciation is only an accounting convention, and bears no direct relationship to new investment requirements in any particular period. Moreover, technology as well as prices may change, with the result that assets are replaccd by a higher level of technology and efficiency. At the same time the company's stock of assets may be increasing, so that the proportionate requirement for asset replacement diminishes, offsetting inflation. Again the new investment outlay will depend upon the age and condition of the company's assets. And finally, the rate of price increase of fixed assets is normally well below that of general consumer inflation. For all these reasons depreciation provision is so complicated that a single simple adjustment for inflation cannot be expected to produce a 'true' figure.

(ii) *Working capital:*

Inflation can also cause profits to rise due to a rise in the value of stocks, known as stock appreciation. It is argued that these are really only paper profits, as the replacement of these stocks has to be undertaken at the higher prices. Again, however, there are several offsetting factors.

The rise in stock values may not correspond to the general rate of consumer price inflation; companies may anticipate rising replacement costs of stocks in their pricing policies; and adroit purchasing policies and timing as well as any physical increase in volume of stocks can add to profits in a very real sense alongside any paper gain from stock appreciation. (A real example of the possibilities in this respect is to be found in the Appendix to the Evidence on Page 71 of this Note).

It is probable that amounts outstanding in the form of debtors will also rise along with inflation, and will need to be financed either by extra borrowing or from retained profits. Here it is worth remembering that one firm's debtors are another firm's creditors, so that there will be gainers as well as losers from this tendency.

(iii) *Borrowing:*

Inflation will cause companies with overall net monetary assets to lose, and those with net monetary liabilities to gain. Thus, where assets are financed by a loan, the rise in their value due to inflation will accrue to the equity shareholders, not to the lender. In this way a company can protect the value of the equity by increased borrowing in times of inflation, though there are risks of illiquidity and of too high a level of capital gearing beyond a certain point, so that companies cannot totally pass on the burden of inflation to lenders.

(iv) *Taxation:*

It has been argued that companies would have lower tax liabilities if allowance were made for inflation, since profits would be lower or even non-existent on the adjusted basis. However, it is worth noting here that until the recent introduction of advance corporation tax, the whole of a company's tax was payable only after a time-lag of up to a couple of years, and also that inflation has been allowed for in the setting of the corporation tax rate at a low level and with high tax allowances.

It can thus be seen that although inflation has very wide effects upon companies, there are many offsetting and additional factors which should be taken into account. Thus the CBI's observations appear rather simplistic and not a little biased:

> "In the majority of cases profits show up as greater than they really are with the result that retentions of profits are inadequate for the replacement of fixed assets and the maintenance of working capital in real terms and still more inadequate for expansion of the business. Shareholders are deceived as to the proportion of net profit being paid out as dividends. Governments believe themselves to be taxing profits at a lower rate than they actually are. Unions believe that their members are getting a smaller share of the added value than is the true case. Managements may even be lulled into thinking that the business is healthier than it is."
>
> Source: Inflation and Company Accounts, CBI, January 1973.

*Current Purchasing Power Accounting*

The Institute of Chartered Accountants in England and Wales (ICA) issued in May 1974 a Provisional Statement of standard accounting practice on "Accounting for Changes in the Purchasing Power of Money". It is provisional in that the Inflation Accounting Committee set up by the Government is not due to report until 1975, but its recommendation that firms should produce supplementary statements with figures adjusted for inflation is being followed by companies currently.

The method proposed is that the statement should be expressed in terms of pounds of purchasing power at the end of the year to which the accounts relate. The conversion should be performed according to the movement in the Department of Employment's Retail Price Index (though in their original Exposure Draft of January 1973 on this subject the ICA recommended use of the Central Statistical Office's Consumer Price Index). Monetary items in the balance sheet at the end of the year will remain the same as they are in the orthodox accounts, whilst non-monetary items are to be increased in proportion to inflation since their acquisition or revaluation. The difference between the total equity interest in the converted balance sheets at the beginning and end of the year (after allowing for dividends and the introduction of new capital) is the profit or loss measured in pounds of purchasing power at the end of the year.

It is important to distinguish the current purchasing power approach from replacement cost accounting. The latter does not attempt to adjust for the effects of general inflation, but rather to adjust for specific price changes, arising for any reason, which affect the company. The ICA makes this distinction, but rejects the replacement cost approach as too broad and subjective. It might be argued however (and indeed is in the Annual Report of Wedgwood Ltd. with which we open our Evidence) that replacement cost accounting is more realistic.

Our detailed criticisms of current purchasing power accounting as proposed by the ICA are to be found in our Evidence below. It only remains for us to consider the nature and scale of the adjustments which arise.

### *Implications of current purchasing power accounting*

There are two spheres of interest here: the relative effects of the adjustments *between* industries, and *within* an industry. As far as the former is concerned, we reproduce on page 62 of our Evidence a Table from the Phillips and Drew Study "Accounting for Inflation", which shows clearly how manufacturing companies' profitability is generally downgraded by inflation accounting, whilst the earnings of many services, especially property, are enhanced by the adjustments.

The most comprehensive study of inflation accounting for one industry is probably the Mechanical Engineering EDC's "Inflation and Company Accounts in Mechanical Engineering". After applying the adjustments for the period 1965-1971, the EDC found that profits in mechanical engineering had been substantially overstated, due mainly to stock appreciation but also partly to under-provision for the replacement of assets. At the same time there was some offsetting relief in the form of additional profits arising from companies' greater net monetary liability.

The EDC's main conclusions were:

| *Item* | *Unadjusted* | *Adjusted* |
|---|---|---|
| Return on capital employed, 1966-1971 | 12.5% to 13.8% | 9.5% to 10% |
| Tax as % of profits after interest | 41% | 53% |
| Increase in total assets 1965-71 | 53% | 18% |
| Real increase in equity stake 1965-71 | 26% | 5% |
| Increase in pre-tax pre-interest profits, 1966-1971 | 57% | 13% |

The rest of this Note consists of the TURU Evidence to the Inflation Accounting Committee, and the connected correspondence.

*Trade Union Research Unit Evidence to the Inflation Accounting Committee*

Extract from the Chairman's statement of Wedgwood Limited, Annual Report 1974:

*"Inflation 'accounting'*

Pages 30 and 31 are included to give effect to the recommendations of the Institute of Chartered Accountants in England and Wales but for no other reason. The results of using the retail price index to adjust a widely varying range of revenue and capital items in divergent industries in different parts of the country over widely extended periods of time will provide no sensible basis of comparative performance. If any form of inflation accounting will do anything but encourage inflation, which is open to doubt, it would have to be more soundly based than the present proposals. The possibility of this, after several millenniums of inflation, is remote. There would be merit in a realistic approach to the problem by providing depreciation on relatively short-life assets (perhaps ten years would be a sensible term) at replacement cost provided this system was followed to its logical conclusion and tax relief granted on the true replacement cost. Any investment analyst who forms a view of Wedgwood from pages 30 and 31 will almost certainly arrive at a misleading verdict."

Whilst there can be no doubt that inflation has a wide-ranging impact on the performance of companies, we are inclined towards the view expressed above as far as the adequacy of inflation accounting on the basis of "current purchasing power" as recommended by the Institute of Chartered Accountants is concerned. Our reservations fall under the following headings:

i) the general validity of the "current purchasing power" approach;
ii) the importance of stock and asset valuation;

iii) the distinction between profitability and liquidity;
iv) the choice of price index;
v) practical problems, especially the treatment of overseas subsidiaries;
vi) the reality of administered pricing;
vii) the question of 'equivalence' within a collective bargaining context;
viii) the importance of other forms of informational requirements on the part of trade unions.

Each set of reservations is described in turn below.

i) *The general validity of the "current purchasing power" approach*

The impact of inflation upon company performance is not a uniform influence, either between different companies or between different element of company accounts. Indeed, the Institute of Chartered Accountants (ICA) begin to justify their approach with the claim that:

> "It is important that managements and other users of financial accounts should be in a position to appreciate the effects of inflation on the businesses with which they are concerned – for example, the effects on costs, profits, distribution policies, dividend cover, the exercise of borrowing powers, returns on funds and future cash needs."
>
> Source: ICA Explanatory Note Para.3.

This list represents only some of the aspects of company affairs affected by inflation, but it can readily be seen that it is a very diverse one: the considerations are qualitatively and conceptually quite different. Thus, costs and profits are elements of actual past company performance; distribution policies, dividend cover and the exercise of borrowing powers are reflections of the exercise of choice between distributed and retained profits and to a great extent of capital gearing; future cash needs and borrowing policies again will be determined by investment policies as well as past performance; and returns on funds represent the result of a whole amalgum of these and other elements. To attempt to "correct" all these different kinds of features of company performance, policy, and prospects with a single uniform method of adjustment can only be misleading, because they are qualitatively different, because they are all vitally affected by factors other than inflation (e.g., depreciation policies, which are themselves influenced by the availability and terms of grants and tax allowances from government) and because they represent different platforms of interest in company affairs (management approach, shareholders' interest, investment appraisal, stock market standing, etc.). For all these reasons the diversity of the list does not lend itself to the current purchasing power approach, which can only be a simplistic, arbitrary and partial adjustment process.

These observations become even more valid when comparisons *between* companies (especially those in different economic sectors), as opposed to accounting analysis *within* a company, are considered. An analysis by the stockbrokers Phillips and Drew is of interest here ("Accounting for Inflation", P.W. Parker and P.M.D. Gibbs). This study indicated that whilst the *median* change in company profits in 1972 resulting from the "inflation accounting" adjustment process would be a reduction of 15%, there would be a very wide range around this figure:

*How Company Earnings would change with inflation accounting*

| | % | | % |
|---|---|---|---|
| Property | + 310 | Light Electronics, etc. | - 15 |
| Entertainment, catering | + 40 | Tobacco | - 15 |
| Breweries | + 35 | Food Manufacturing | - 20 |
| Miscellaneous (other groups) | + 5 | Office Equipment | - 25 |
| Stores | + 5 | Oil | - 25 |
| Food retailing | + 5 | Household Goods | - 35 |
| Newspapers, Publishing | - 10 | Packaging and Paper | - 35 |
| Contracting, Construction | - 10 | Shipping | - 40 |
| Building Materials | - 10 | Miscellaneous (capital) | - 40 |
| Hire Purchase | - 15 | Engineering (heavy) | - 40 |
| Banks | - 15 | Textiles | - 50 |
| Chemicals | - 15 | Engineering (general) | - 50 |
| Wines and Spirits | - 15 | Electricals | - 50 |
| | | Motor & Distributors | - 60 |

The median change is – 15%, equivalent to a pre-tax change of -7½%.

The implication of inflation accounting is thus that practically all manufacturing companies, and engineering especially, have only been making "paper" profits, whilst many service industries, and property in particular, have been understating their true profits. The disturbing features of this conclusion are several:

a) investors would be apparently well advised to move out of productive exporting sectors;
b) temporary economic trends affecting stock values are amplified out of all proportion when "corrected" for inflation within the context of profitability;

c) manufacturing companies would see justifications for substantial price increases in the relative figures;
d) the incidence of company taxation, and its distribution between companies, is brought into question.

These implications are so significant, and so closely inter-related with other major economic considerations, that any shift in emphasis from historic cost to current purchasing power accounting needs to be treated with the utmost caution, and certainly not undertaken in isolation from those other considerations.

ii) *The importance of stock and asset valuation*

There are two major reasons why the profitability of many companies would be reduced by the application of inflation accounting:
a) the exclusion of "paper" profits on stock appreciation, and
b) under-provision for the replacement of fixed assets.

a) *Stock appreciation*

The Mechanical Engineering EDC study "Inflation and Company Accounts in Mechanical Engineering" found the former had a relatively greater impact over the years 1966-71 in that sector, and there is no doubt that increases in raw material, commodity and oil prices since then have maintained the importance of this factor for many sectors. However, certain questions arise from the treatment of stock appreciation under inflation accounting.

First, is it legitimate – let alone helpful – to revalue stocks according to a general price index regardless of the way in which they specifically have moved in price terms? This is a particularly important consideration against a background of *falling* input prices (such as non-ferrous metals and animal feeding stuffs currently, which will affect the true values of stocks and work-in-progress in metal-using and food-producing industries). Second, does stock appreciation really represent a mere "paper" gain, and as such be deductable from profits in accounting terms? After all, even under the provisions of the Price Code, increased raw material, etc., prices represent allowable costs, and as such can be passed on by pricing policies, with the result that neither profitability nor liquidity need actually suffer.

b) *Depreciation provision*

The current purchasing power approach to inflation accounting assumes that if assets are revalued in terms of replacement cost rather than historic cost, it follows that the depreciation requirement will be correspondingly higher, with the result that net profits and the return on assets are reduced. Again however several crucial reservations arise.

First, there will be significant differences in the age and quality of assets between industries, between firms within industries, and indeed between the assets themselves within companies. Since the effective working life of assets can also be variable, it is dangerously simplistic to adjust asset values generally according to any standard measure of inflation (least of all the Retail Price Index: a further reservation discussed under (iv) below). Indeed, the Trade Union Research Unit would take this positive and crucial consideration far further, rather than suffocate it with the current purchasing power approach, since studies of the effective working life and average age of different assets in different industries should form a pre-requisite analysis underpinning the provision of government aid to industry through grants and allowances.

Second, and following in part from the first reservation, is the extent to which the current purchasing power approach will frequently overstate the true replacement cost of the asset and/or its true current value to the company. As well as the relationship between the age and effective working life of assets and the actual depreciation provision against them, there is the question of changes in technology. We find it alarming that whilst this key area is treated with extreme caution by both official and academic approaches (see for instance "National Income Accounts: Sources and Methods," HMSO), the ICA summarily dismisses the importance of replacement cost accounting as a "management" rather than a "shareholder" approach. The economist's mind is left with the uneasy impression that the Institute has opted for simplicity rather than suitability (an impression consolidated by the ICA choice of the Retail Price Index as the appropriate adjustment, discussed under (iv) below). The ICA stresses the potential complexity and comprehensiveness of replacement cost accounting in an Appendix to their Provisional Statement of standard accounting practice:

> "In using a replacement cost method, therefore, a wide degree of discretion and subjective judgement enters in each separate case into the choice of the adjustment factor, and a general index for adjustment of asset values cannot be prescribed.
>
> The replacement cost of an asset can rise or fall when there is no change at all in the general price level (i.e. when there is no inflation). Relative price changes may be due to technological, economic, social or legal factors.
>
> The fact that the question of replacement cost is separate from that of CPP correction does not prevent the reporting of information on replacement cost to shareholders where this is considered to be relevant. This can be done, if desired, in a supplementary accounting statement, additional to and separate

from the CPP supplementary statement, or where appropriate by adjustment of the ordinary accounts.

It should be noted, however, that the attempt to make replacement cost adjustments can give rise to very considerable difficulties of calculation and in some cases, e.g. where there is technological change, the result may be virtually meaningless unless the replacement cost is calculated for the whole of a particular industrial complex."

Source: ICA Appendix 1, Paras. 9, 10, 11 & 12.

Whilst these observations correctly recognise the dynamic and specific characteristics of replacement cost accounting, they represent in no way a *justification* for the current purchasing power approach as a superior or more adequate alternative; they merely bear witness to its relative simplicity. Unfortunately this very characteristic is also its greatest weakness, and a potential source of distortion in the context of asset valuation and depreciation provision.

Finally, it is important to note that the logic of the current purchasing power approach requires that investment grants and tax allowances be adjusted proportionately in relation to current values in line with depreciation provision, and that such treatment represents an offsetting factor against any reduction in profits on the inflation-adjusted basis.

iii) *The distinction between profitability and liquidity*

Having noted the two main reasons why the profitability of many companies might be lower under inflation accounting, we now turn our attention to the major offsetting factor. This is the net gain in purchasing power resulting from the effects of inflation upon its net monetary liabilities, i.e., from any excess of long- and short-term indebtedness over debtors and cash. Here the logic of the current purchasing power approach is to suggest a real gain to shareholders notwithstanding the dangers of illiquidity and/or high capital gearing. In such cases, where a company could not possibly distribute the gain without raising additional finance, the distinction between profitability and liquidity is underlined. The ICA draws attention to this, but insists that the accounting principle is correct even though its implications may be misleading:

"*Monetary and non-monetary items*

In converting the figures in the basic historical cost accounts into those in the supplementary current purchasing power statement a distinction is drawn between:

a) monetary items, and
b) non-monetary items.

Monetary items are those whose amounts are fixed by contract or otherwise in terms of numbers of pounds, regardless of changes in general price levels. Examples of monetary items are cash, debtors, creditors and loan capital. Holders of monetary assets lose general purchasing power during a period of inflation to the extent that any income from the assets does not adequately compensate for the loss; the converse applies to those having monetary liabilities. A company with a material excess on average over the year of long- and short-term debt (e.g. debentures and creditors) over debtors and cash will show, in its supplementary current purchasing power statement, a gain in purchasing power during the year. This is a real gain to the equity shareholders in purchasing power but it has to be appreciated that there may be circumstances in which it will be accompanied by a dangerously illiquid situation or by excessively high gearing, and for this reason any such gain should be shown as profit in the supplementary statement because it might not be possible to distribute it without raising additional finance. This argument, however, confuses the measurement of profitability with the measurement of liquidity. Even in the absence of inflation, the whole of a company's profit may not be distributable without raising additional finance, for example because it has been invested in, or earmarked for investment in, non-liquid assets.

Moreover, it is inconsistent to exclude such gains when profit has been debited with the cost of borrowing (which must be assumed to reflect anticipation of inflation by the lender during the currency of the loan), and with depreciation on the converted cost of fixed assets."

Source: ICA Paras. 14 & 17.

It is important to realise, however, that the current purchasing power approach can permit the net liability position of closely similar companies to exercise widely varying influences upon profit figures. The importance of considering a company's liquidity along with its inflation-adjusted accounts cannot therefore be over-emphasised: this represents yet another reason why the current purchasing power approach results cannot be considered in isolation.

### iv) *The choice of price index*

We have already argued that the adjustment of stock and asset values according to a general price index is a highly questionable procedure. Even if the procedure were justified, the choice of the Department of Employment's General Index of Retail Prices (opted for by the ICA) would in our opinion still be quite inappropriate.

The main reason for this view is that the Retail Price Index relates to that proportion of average household income which is actually spent on goods and services, and to the price movements of those goods and services. It is in other words a household consumption price index, the weights for which are only derived from Family Expenditure Survey data *after* high-income households are removed from the sample and *after* all forms of saving and investment (including owner-occupier mortgages) have been excluded. Since Inland Revenue and other sources illustrate clearly that equity shareholders fall predominantly into high-income and large wealth-holding classes, and since equity shareholdings represent a major form of investment or saving, there can surely be no justification for the application of the Retail Price Index to company accounts figures in order to provide a resultant figure for equity interest adjusted for inflation. Equally, there can be no validity is using a general *consumer* price index to adjust the values of *capital* goods and stock held by companies.

Against these serious qualifications, the current purchasing power approach can only provide an artificial indicator of changes in real values as far as company activities and shareholders' interests are concerned. The notion of current purchasing power accounting in effect provides its own conceptual basis:

> "Because current purchasing power accounting is concerned primarily with the effects of inflation on the measurement of the profits of, and the purchasing power invested in an undertaking (e.g. by the equity shareholders in the case of a company, or by the nation as a whole in the case of a public enterprise), it uses a measure of the change in the power of money to purchase commodities of the type that consumers in general buy.
>
> For example, if an individual shareholder wishes to consider how inflation has affected his financial position as between two dates, he will be concerned with the effect on his power to purchase the goods and services he usually buys. No index of changes in the purchasing power of consumers in general is perfect, because people's tastes and purchasing patterns differ. As in other human affairs, a workable approximation has to be used. Statisticians have given a great deal of thought to devising indices that will provide a good indication of the effect of general price changes on consumers. The retail price index has been selected for CPP adjustments because it is regarded as the best available indicator of changes in the general purchasing power of money to consumers".
>
> Source: ICA Appendix 1, Paras. 3 & 4.

It seems to us an unconvincing step from the original objective of adjusting company accounts for the effects of inflation, to the intermediate concern with a generalised current purchasing power approach and to the particular choice of the Retail Price Index for the purposes of adjustment. Companies are not households, and the "average" shareholder can in no way be equated with the "average" household. The measure of changes in purchasing power provided by the movement in the Retail Price Index is only meaningful in the context of the average family's expenditure pattern; outside this context it can be no more than a convenient indicator. Perhaps it is for reasons of convenience that the ICA opts for the Retail Price Index as its basis for adjusting for inflation.

Finally, it is worth mentioning that even within its more conventional sphere of usage the Retail Price Index has severe limitations and inadequacies (fully documented in the Trade Union Research Unit's "Technical Notes for Bargainers"). We doubt whether the ICA are aware of all these additional factors which detract from the value and applicability of the Index; indeed, they fail to mention in their list of sources for the Retail Price Index the original, major and most detailed source, the Department of Employment Gazette.

v) *Practical problems, particularly the treatment of overseas subsidiaries*

In the light of our arguments under (iv) above, we would have to regard the choice and application of an appropriate index as the most difficult practical problem, but there are others too.

The main one is the procedure to be adopted with regard to the adjustment of the figures of overseas subsidiaries and associated companies, which the ICA do not in our opinion face up to:

> "*Overseas subsidiaries and associates*
>
> It is possible that some companies may experience difficulties in obtaining the information necessary to produce the current purchasing power supplementary statements from some of their overseas subsidiaries or associates. In such cases, directors will have to weigh the materiality of the items concerned against the cost of obtaining the necessary information. The reasons for the treatment adopted and the magnitude of the items involved, should be disclosed in a note to the supplementary statement."
>
> Source: ICA Appendix 1, Para. 27.

The CBI document "Inflation and Company Accounts" is more forthcoming in acknowledging the very real and wide-ranging difficulties involved:

> "There are obvious difficulties with subsidiary and associated companies overseas. If it is accepted that in the longer term cross rates of exchange reflect the relative degrees of inflation between countries, in the view of the Committee overseas assets etc. to sterling at the rates ruling at the time of acquisition and indices and converted to sterling at current rates of exchange. On occasions, however, it may be necessary to use the alternative method of converting overseas assets etc. to sterling at the rates ruling at the time of acquisition and then adjusting for changes in UK current purchasing power indices.
>
> Anomalies will arise when, in the short term, cross rates are not representative of commercial reality and there may be difficulties if representative indices are not available in the overseas country. Difficulties may arise in obtaining the necessary analyses of overseas assets, as to dates of acquisition and disposal, for the initial restatement calculations, and acceptable short cut methods and common-sense will be required. It is the opinion that most if not all companies with overseas operations already have the data and mechanics for making these adjustments."
>
> Source: CBI Para. 5.2.4.

but the CBI too similarly skate over the practical implications:

> "If indices are to be applied to overseas assets before conversion to sterling, the same basic treatment should be adopted as for UK assets. The choice of the most representative foreign index should be left to the discretion of the companies."
>
> Source: CBI Para. 5.2.6.

It is only when one turns to the Text and Tables of the ICA's "Accounting for Inflation: a working guide to the accounting procedures" that the full dimensions of the task are indicated, and many pages are taken up with explanatory notes and figures.

Whilst the ICA's recommendations on inflation accounting are intended only initially for the annual accounts of listed companies, it is of course amongst these that "multinational" companies are to be found. It is for these that the task of inflation accounting in respect of overseas subsidiaries and associates is at its most daunting, but where the necessity for its being undertaken is greatest. Whilst a company like Wedgwood is able to avoid the problems by

> "using the United Kingdom index as it is considered that the use of appropriate overseas indices would not materially affect the conversion", (Wedgwood 1974 Annual Report, Page 31)

this would hardly be a satisfactory approach for a company such as, say, Coats Patons, which provides 64% of its world sales from production outside the UK.

vi) *The reality of administered pricing*

The current purchasing power approach to inflation accounting implies that companies are passive victims of, as opposed to transmitters and initiators of, inflation. Nothing could be further from the truth in an economy in which administered pricing is the rule (broadly speaking, full-cost as opposed to marginal-cost pricing policies predominate). Companies are continually passing on their increased costs, the direct or indirect consequences of inflation, into prices, with a shortening time-lag in correlation to accelerating inflation. Moreover, companies include an 'anticipatory' element in their administered prices based on expectations about future inflation, as well as reflecting past and current cost increases. Whilst the application of a Price Code may to some degree circumscribe the freedom of company pricing policies, it is undoubtedly the case that companies are responding to and allowing for inflation, and thus that any approach to inflation accounting will be over-compensating for the effects of inflation. This is particularly so if the transmission process between costs and prices does not occur within a single accounting year.

vii) *"Equivalence" within a collective bargaining context*

If attempts to adjust the accounts – and particularly the profits – of companies for the effects of inflation are justified, then the principle must be extended to other elements in collective bargaining too, notably labour productivity and employee remuneration. *Real* productivity, as the relationship between output or added value and the labour input or its remuneration, must be disclosed by companies. The Trade Union Research Unit's experience is that companies are acutely reticent on this score.

Equally, companies must acknowledge the significance of the *real disposable income* remaining to their employees from their gross earnings or standard wage rates; again the Trade Union Research Unit has experienced a distinct lack of enthusiasm on the part of employers for approaching pay bargaining on this basis.

Against these considerations the CBI's rather simplistic qualms about employee attitudes towards the impact of inflation can be seen to fall a long way short of these central requirements:

> *"Effect on a company's pricing policy*
>
> On the one hand managements that have not appreciated the true position are likely to increase their prices to restore the true profit position insofar as competition permits. If widespread, this would tend to raise the cost of living, and so to lead to pressure for higher wages. On the other hand historical accounting overstates profit which in turn stimulates wage demands. Knowledge of a company's true position should be an essential factor in negotiations with trade unions."
>
> Source: CBI Para. 5.1.3.

The Trade Union Research Unit fully endorses this last sentence, as a principle worthy of general application to company performance in the context of collective bargaining. Our worry here is that the CBI member companies perhaps do not share this conviction with the CBI and ourselves. This leads us into the final heading of our reservations on inflation accounting: the question of disclosure of company information.

viii) *The importance of other forms of informational requirements on the part of trade unions.*

Whilst not denying the significant impact which inflation can have upon a company's activities, we are not sure that inflation accounting would be all that high in the order of trade union priorities with respect to the disclosure of company information for collective bargaining.

The TUC have, in several publications, presented lists of informational requirements not hitherto supported either by Companies Acts or by negotiating conventions; many of these requirements were endorsed as being consistent with "good industrial relations practice" by the Commission of Industrial Relations' Report on "Disclosure of Information." Suffice it to say here that data in the fields of manpower, costs, productivity, ownership structure, and investment are of far more pressing concern for trade unions than any rather questionable attempts to adjust published accounts for inflation. In other words, unions are more eager for extensions and developments of information in company accounts, and additional items of information thereto, than they are with a generalised adjustment process to already limited and arbitrary published figures. Moreover, unions will not be convinced of a company's "true" position as inferred by accounts on a current purchasing power basis provided in isolation from these other higher priorities for disclosure. To expect otherwise would be like translating a partial and inadequate description of a complicated process into a foreign language in the hope that it would provide elucidation.

References to ICA are taken from "Accounting for changes in the purchasing power of money", Provisional statement of standard accounting practice No. 7. May 1974 issued by the Institute of Chartered Accountants in England and Wales.

*Appendix to Evidence: The Reality of Cost Movements*

This Appendix is attached to our main evidence in order to provide an actual example of the inadequacy of the current purchasing power approach to inflation accounting in the context of what is really happening to the price of an important commodity.

The following price indices for *raw cotton* (completely imported and free from price control under the Price Code), have been derived from Tables 5 and 10 of the article "Activity in the Textiles and Clothing Industries" in *Trade and Industry*, 25 April 1974:

*Price of raw cotton, 1972 = 100*

| *1973* | *Direct Imports* | *Home sales of imports* |
|---|---|---|
| 1st Quarter | 97 | 115 |
| 2nd Quarter | 106 | 132 |
| 3rd Quarter | 123 | 212 |
| 4th Quarter | 160 | 242 |

The difference in price movements is very substantial, and provides two crucial factors which will determine the true stock appreciation experienced by any textiles or associated company:

1) the timing of its acquisition of raw cotton; and
2) whether it is acquiring imported cotton directly (as will most large textile companies and merchants) or buying domestically from merchants' stocks.

The simple adjustment which would meet the Institute of Chartered Accountants' recommendations would be to calculate the

> "additional charge based on restating the cost of stock at the beginning and end of the year in pounds of current purchasing power, thus taking the inflationary element out of the profit on the sale of stocks" (ICA Appendix 2, page 16)

and then to adjust the original profit figure downwards by this amount. This operation would be based on the movement in the Retail Price Index during 1973.

It can readily be seen that nothing could be more likely to misrepresent what companies were in fact experiencing as far as stock appreciation is concerned, particularly any company or merchant which bought imports of raw cotton early in 1973 for re-sale or conversion later in the year.

Such circumstances as these are merely hinted at, and then submerged, in that approach to inflation accounting which is based upon current purchasing power. For instance, the Mechanical Engineering EDC study of "Inflation and Company Accounts in Mechanical Engineering" states on page 19 under the heading "Inflation and Working Capital":

> "Inflation also creates purely paper profits arising from stock appreciation and at the same time results in increased requirements of working capital. A rise in the value of stocks due to inflation normally inflates profits by the amount of the rise. But to the extent that the profits increase reflects simply the rising replacement cost of stocks rather than skilful purchasing or an increase in the volume of business, the gain is a paper gain only; the profit will be fully absorbed in keeping stocks at their original volume in the face of higher prices. A truer figure for profits is obtained if the contribution of inflation to the rise in the value of stocks is deducted."

We very much doubt whether, in circumstances such as those above, this is in fact the case.

*Correspondence between Inflation Accounting Committee and TURU*
From Inflation Accounting Committee, St. Helen's, 1 Undershaft, London EC3P 3DQ.

To: J. Hughes, Esq., Director, Trade Union Research Unit, Ruskin College, Oxford.

21st May, 1974

Dear Mr. Hughes,

I am writing on behalf of the Inflation Accounting Committee to ask if you would be good enough to assist us on certain points that have arisen during our discussions.

The Inflation Accounting Committee is an independent Committee of Enquiry set up by the previous Government, under the Chairmanship of Mr. F.E.P. Sandilands, to consider whether, and if so how, company accounts should allow for changes in costs and prices. I attach a copy of the full terms of references of the Committee and also a list of its members.

You will see that among the matters the Committee is required to take into account are the requirements of investors, creditors, employees, Government and public. We understand that you have assisted a number of Trade Unions in preparing for wage negotiations with employers, and we should be very grateful for your views on the merits and drawbacks of the existing form of company accounts as a source of information for this work. In particular we should be interested in your views on the following points:

i) What use do you make of the published accounts of companies in your work?

ii) What are the main pieces of information you hope to obtain from company accounts?

iii) To what extent do company accounts fail to provide this required information because they do not allow adequately for changes in costs and prices?

iv) If you consider it would be helpful to show the effect of changes in costs and prices in company accounts, how could this best be done to meet your requirements? In particular what are your views on the method proposed in Standard Statement of Accounting Practice No.7., issued this month by the Institute of Chartered Accountants in England and Wales.

In order that we may press ahead with our task as quickly as possible we should be very grateful if you could try to let us have your views on these points within the next month. The Committee may subsequently wish to invite you to discuss your views at a meeting.

We may at a later stage wish to publish some of the evidence we receive but we shall not, of course, do so without the agreement of those concerned.

I very much hope you will be able to assist us in this way. If you would like any further information, please let me know.

Yours sincerely,
M.J. Mitchell,
Secretary.

## THE COMMITTEE ON COMPANY ACCOUNTS AND INFLATION

*Terms of Reference*

"To consider whether, and if so how, company accounts should allow for changes (including relative changes) in costs and prices, having regard to established accounting conventions based on historic costs, the proposal for current general purchasing power accounting put forward by the Accounting Standards Steering Committee, and other possible accounting methods of allowing for price changes, and to make recommendations. In considering the question the following matters, inter alia, should be taken into account –

i) the effects upon investment and other management decisions, and upon the efficiency of companies generally
ii) the effect on the efficient allocation of resources through the capital market
iii) the need to restrain inflation in the United Kingdom
iv) the requirements of investors, creditors, employees, Government and the public for information
v) any implications for the taxation of the profits and capital gains of companies, the assumption being that the share of the total direct tax burden borne by the company sector remains unchanged
vi) the repercussions on the accounts of other corporate bodies
vii) procedures in other countries particularly EEC."

## MEMBERS OF THE SANDILANDS COMMITTEE

Chairman:

| | | |
|---|---|---|
| Mr. F.E.P. Sandilands | – | Chairman of Commercial Union Assurance., |

Members:

| | | |
|---|---|---|
| Lord Caldecote | – | Chairman, Delta Metal Co. Ltd., |
| Mr. D.R. Chilvers | – | Partner in Coopers & Lybrand., |
| Lord Feather | – | President of the European Trade Union Confederation., |
| Mr. M.A. Inwards | – | Financial Controller, Pye Unicam, Ltd., |
| Mr. E. Kaye | – | Chairman and Governing Director, Lansing-Bagnall Ltd., |
| Mr. A.J.W.S. Leonard | – | Director, Shell International Petroleum Ltd., |
| Mrs. C.M. Miles | – | Financial and Economic Consultant |
| Mr. M.P. Nolan Q.C. | | |
| Professor W. Reid | – | London Graduate School of Business Studies |
| Mr. P. Shelbourne | – | Chairman, Drayton Group Ltd., |
| Professor R. Turvey | – | Economic Advisor to Scientific Control Systems Ltd. |

---

From the Trade Union Research Unit Ruskin College, Oxford.
To: Mr. M.J. Michell, Secretary, Inflation Accounting Committee, St. Helen's, 1 Undershaft, London EC3P 3DQ.

Dear Mr Michell,

I am sorry to be late in responding fully to your letter of 21 May 1974 reference IAC/L.20, but have preferred to wait until our working timetable and resources permit a thorough and detailed response to your inquiries. I am now able to enclose a document representing our evidence to the Inflation Accounting Committee (which will be circulated, together with an introduction to the subject, to our affiliated trade unions).

The specific questions which you raise in your letter are, we hope, answered within our evidence, but it might be helpful if I set out the following additional points in response to the four questions raised:

i) We make considerable use of the published accounts of companies in our work, both in the context of pay negotiations and collective bargaining generally (e.g. The Ford and I.C.I. wage claims, submitted over the past three years by the Transport and General Workers Union); and in general research such as Industrial Studies and analysis of multinational companies and their operations.

ii) As far as collective bargaining is concerned, we would normally attempt to assess a company's performance over recent years, and to project forward to an assessment of current and likely future performance. We are particularly interested in any guidance on productivity and profitability which the accounts can provide; in implications for investment and manpower policies; and in the adequacy of sales, marketing and exports. Finally we are interested in movements in costs and prices and in changes in production levels and capacity utilisation.

As far as more general research is concerned, we would often additionally be interested in the trading and ownership relations between companies, and in more detail on their subsidiaries abroad.

However, in any research work of this nature we would never consider the accounts of companies out of the context of wider data on the industry and product markets in which they operate.

iii) Our research work is hindered far more by the very limited provision in company accounts of data of relevance to subjects of trade union concern than by any failure of companies to allow for the impact of inflation. We are also restricted on many occasions by the inadequate degree of detail and by misleading presentation of figures within company accounts, quite apart from any additional complications thrown up by inflation.

iv) We are critical of the specific approach chosen by the Institute of Chartered Accountants to adjust company accounts for inflation; our accompanying evidence describes our reservations in detail.

I hope that this evidence will be of some assistance to the Inflation Accounting Committee, and apologise for not having been in a position to submit our views any earlier.

Yours sincerely,

R.E. Moore,
Research Officer.

# PART TWO

## Evidence on the Distribution of Income and Wealth

# Statement by Jack Jones

We have already appeared before you in connection with our Evidence on the Company Income Reference, and we welcome this opportunity today to expand upon our Evidence related to the Standing Reference. Our written submission has been perhaps even more technical and detailed than before, but this is unavoidable if a serious study of the distribution of income and wealth is to be undertaken. It is possible, however, to single out certain main themes which emerge from our evidence, and to identify the kind of action required to remedy both the inadequacies and inequities.

Indeed, it is towards inadequacies and inequities that our Evidence addresses itself: the inadequacies of our knowledge of the true facts of income and wealth distribution, and the inequities of the pattern which emerges when the available facts are put together. What we hope will be forthcoming from the Report of this Royal Commission are immediate and practical proposals to deal with the gaps in our knowledge of the real position as far as income and wealth are concerned; acknowledgement of the gross inequities which exist – and which indeed have been encouraged by Conservative governments; and indications as to the kind of measures and policies required if the degree of inequality is to be reduced.

We are convinced that the picture of income and wealth distribution derived from Inland Revenue data is deficient and misleading on many accounts, and in *Section One* we give our reasons. All definitions are those used for tax purposes, so that the only income recorded is the *taxable* income of *tax units* above the *tax threshold,* which means that no measure of the overall distribution, or changes therein, can be derived in an economic sense from Inland Revenue figures. Moreover, we cannot derive any picture of the pattern of lifetime income, which may well provide evidence of even sharper inequalities.

Notwithstanding these inadequacies, the picture which emerges over the post-war period is that such redistribution of pre-tax incomes as has occurred has operated in favour of those near the top of the pyramid, as opposed to those in the middle or at the bottom. The top five per cent continue to receive nearly twice as much income in total as the bottom thirty per cent (Tables 2 and 3, page 93).

As far as personal wealth is concerned, the degree of inequality is greater still than for incomes, with 10% of wealth holders holding over half of all personal wealth. However, since half the adult population hold no dutiable wealth at all, the actual degree of inequality is sharper still. Indeed, when various necessary adjustments are made to the Inland Revenue wealth figures, there has been little or no redistribution of wealth over recent years. As with the distribution of income, any redistribution of wealth has not benefited those at the bottom.

There is a two-way relationship between taxation and information on income and wealth. On the one hand, such information as we do have comes from the Inland Revenue; it is based upon their definitions and affected by people's ability to avoid or minimise their tax liability (an ability far greater for the rich than for the ordinary worker). On the other hand, adequate information about incomes and wealth has to be a pre-condition of more effective taxation; this will be particularly true for the wealth tax and the capital transfer tax.

Our concern about these grotesque inequalities, and about the deficiences of our official information, does not derive solely from considerations of fairness, important though these are. We are also conscious of the immense power and control that large holdings of wealth – particularly in the form of stocks and shares – can bestow upon the holder. As Britain's largest trade union we see this as a source of arbitrary and insufficiently accountable influence exercised by the few over the many.

This then is why we have stressed in our *Section One* the inequalities of income and wealth as well as the inadequacies of our knowledge about the true position. We stress that all income and wealth must be accountable, and that the principles of taxation should be based upon "command over economic resources". We were therefore pleased to see our views echoed recently by the Financial Secretary to the Treasury Mr. Joel Barnett. Speaking at a CBI conference (reported in *Financial Times*, 25 March) he said that:

> "in round terms" it was now estimated that in 1973 1 per cent of the population owned 25 to 30 per cent of the nation's capital, and the top 5 per cent of wealth-holders had 45 to 55 per cent.

Mr. Barnett also reiterated that one advantage from an annual wealth tax could be a reduction in the high rates of tax on income. A measure of taxable capacity which included wealth would be fairer.

We endorse this without reservation.

So far we have only talked in terms of pre-tax income and wealth; it is also necessary to consider the extent to which the system in this country has been used to redistribute incomes, and whether this has been effective when attempted. Our evidence on this (in *Section Two*) is first that tax burdens have increased most for the lowest-paid over the past twenty years. A low-paid worker on two-thirds of average earnings now pays three times the proportion of his income in tax, than he did twenty years ago. The rise in tax liability for the high-paid executive on twenty times average earnings has risen less than one-tenth over the same period. Second, this tendency has acted particularly severely against families with two or more children. Third, our evidence shows clearly that the progressiveness of our tax structure diminished each time a Conservative administration was in office; changes in taxes designed to redistribute income in favour of the lower end were only effective under Labour. Clearly, Labour governments have a considerable way to go in reversing the tendency of previous Conservative administrations before they can actually *advance* the degree of progressiveness.

Nevertheless, our evidence shows that redistribution through the tax system can potentially be achieved given Government commitment and suitable tax policies. We indicate in our evidence the kind of policies needed on tax thresholds, tax rates, and national insurance contributions if progress is to be made towards a fairer distribution of post-tax incomes. We have to emphasise here that the development of comprehensive taxation of wealth as well as more progressiveness in the income tax structure has a key role to play in this respect. We trust that the Royal Commission will be giving due consideration to the role of taxation. But it is not just a question of spreading the *existing* tax burden more fairly; we must also ensure that the many methods of evading and avoiding tax liability are investigated and closed up. We are aware of quite alarming examples of techniques used to make the Inland Revenue's task more difficult. The tendency for individuals to turn themselves into one-man companies was described by Titmuss in 1962; it is a tendency still very much with us today. We refer also in our Evidence to differences in the tax treatment of the self-employed as compared to employees. The latter are taxed on an immediate PAYE basis, whilst the self-employed, on the basis of their own returns, pay their tax some eighteen months in arrears.

Perhaps the most notorious example of the abuse of the tax system by a category of the "self-employed" is "the lump", the very existence of which is owed to the potential tax advantages of the self-employed as compared to the situation of employees.

It is also well known that many self-employed, along with richer individuals and small – often family – companies, resort to a wide variety of methods to minimise or avoid completely their proper tax liability. The use of all kinds of allowances against income, the payment of "fees" and "expenses" to associates and relatives, the artificial creation of directorships – all these and many more provide opportunities for those, whose tax liability would otherwise be much greater, in effect to contribute very little.

A striking example concerns the existence of hidden bank accounts, which could no longer remain if clearing banks were obliged to inform the Inland Revenue of their existence.

This loophole was clearly illustrated by Mr. M.G. Christopher of the Inland Revenue Staff Federation when he addressed the Trades Union Congress in 1974. Mr. Christopher gave the following examples and I quote:

> "First, the case of W, who was a scrap metal merchant. Our inquiry branch discovered a cheque for £1,800 payable to him to a bank account that we knew nothing about. He denied the existence of the other bank account. But our suspicions grew when we discovered he insured a Rolls-Royce, a Mercedes Benz and several thousand pounds worth of jewellery. When his story that the cars came from wealthy lady friends (there's arrogance for you!) broke down he disclosed two hidden bank accounts which revealed omitted profits of nearly £500,000. It is not just the scrap metal merchants. B. was a solicitor. For eight years an accountant sent in perfectly respectable looking accounts showing a growing and successful practice. The Revenue became suspicious and discovered false records of cash payments. They discovered that his gardeners were described as "outside clerks". The Revenue at every stage met total resistance. In fact, he said they could only examine his books once they had got permission to do so, at night when the staff had left. It required the Revenue to call 63 witnesses and 500 exhibits to get £45,000 from him. I have another case where at the end of the day the tax paid was £133,000 resulting from profits taken from the business.
>
> We are fighting a losing battle because we have not the tools to do the job."

This is indicative of the extent to which professional bodies such as banks and accountants are able to obstruct the Inland Revenue from exercising the spirit as well as the letter of tax law. One need not look far to see the growth of the tax avoidance industry: almost daily advertisements in the financial press offer advice, services, conferences, etc., the central purpose of which is to assist both individuals and companies to find more and more holes in the mesh of the tax net.

Legislation is clearly required to ensure that proper records are kept to enable the Inland Revenue to assess proper tax liability, and to ensure adequate access where necessary.

The inequalities to which we draw attention are even greater if non-monetary benefits – "fringe benefits" are taken into account. In *Section Three* of our Evidence we list and describe the main types of benefit which accrue to those already well placed in terms of monetary income. The list is awesome, including generous pension provision, medical care, housing, cars, share options, holidays, etc., and we estimate that the total benefit in monetary terms for an executive can be over £4,000. This of course is on a tax-free basis; at high incomes the pre-tax equivalent becomes a very large sum indeed. We feel it is quite unfair that fringe benefits accrue on a tax-free basis to already highly paid personnel. Our members become especially aggravated when they read of the scale of "golden handshakes" given to outgoing directors whose competence in the circumstances has to be questionable, and when they compare this with the arbitrary manner and minimal severance pay which accompany their own loss of employment through no fault of their own. The "two nations" are indeed still with us.

In considering directors and executives we are again conscious of the power and control, as well as the high incomes and fringe benefits, which are associated with these positions. We are particularly concerned over the existence of substantial multi-directorships, and would insist that all such interests – and the monetary and non-monetary remuneration attaching to them – should be obligatory disclosure requirements under company law (as we argued in *Section Five* of our Company Income evidence).

The picture which emerges then, is of gross inequalities of income and wealth; of substantial gaps in our knowledge and in their accountability; of amplifications of these inequalities of income and control through fringe benefits and interlocking directorships; and of a general failure of our income tax system to remedy these inequities. We go on in *Section Four* to expand on further deficiencies and aspects of inequality, giving particular attention to the overall picture of income distribution when all forms of taxes and benefits are taken into account. Again we are alarmed at inadequacies and inconsistencies in the official treatment and presentation of figures, particularly since the question of the "social wage" is assuming a new relevance under the social contract. Notwithstanding these limitations, the official figures confirm our findings in earlier sections that lower-income families have not fared well in post-war years.

There are many improvements and changes we would like to see in this and other areas of government statistics, all of which can take us towards a more realistic picture of what is really happening to income and wealth distribution. For example, we want to see profiles of annual earnings as well as figures for a single pay-week and we need indices of movements in real take-home pay at different income levels and for different family composition. Our suspicion is that a whole range of factors – the impact of inflation on both purchasing power and tax liability, the tax structure, national insurance contributions, indirect taxes and means-tested benefits – have all acted particularly adversely upon the lower-paid worker and his family.

As a trade union we seek to do a great deal, through both collective bargaining and policy formulation, to advance the relative position of the low-paid worker, but the influences I have just listed mean that they have to run to stand still. A good illustration of this is contained in our Appendix on Equal Pay for Women, which shows the many powerful tendencies which have to be overcome if equal pay is to become a reality, and not merely a statutory formality.

It has been argued that adequate statistics on income and wealth will only be forthcoming if political and social attitudes elevate inequality into a priority area of concern and policy action. We have sought in our Evidence not only to identify the scale and nature of the inequalities which exist, but also to indicate (particularly in *Sections Four* and *Five*) the kind of improvements which could be made in obtaining and presenting more official information on income and wealth. Such information must be reliable and comprehensive if income and wealth are to be accountable and progress towards reducing inequalities is to be made.

The Transport and General Workers Union regard these papers presented to the Royal Commission as evidence of inequalities and inadequacies, and also as evidence of our concern that progress must be made in remedying them. If the principle of a social contract is to gain lasting support from our members and from workers in general, which it must if it is to have any chance of attaining its economic and social objectives, then evidence must be forthcoming in future of serious and effective steps towards exposing the true degree of inequalities in our society, and towards reducing them. We are hopeful that the Royal Commission will recognise the highly significant role which they can play here, and that they will take due account of the analyses, arguments and recommendations which we have placed before them.

# Introduction

This Evidence is not intended to be fully detailed or comprehensive. We selected those areas which concern us most for our attention, and left areas which we are confident will receive the attention of those more expert than ourselves. We have attempted to provide references for other studies wherever relevant, and also to draw out implications and practical proposals wherever possible. In the light of these introductory considerations, we would affirm our readiness to offer supplementary evidence in written or verbal form in the future.

In *Section 1: The Existing Evidence* we review post-war data on income and wealth distribution and indicate the overwhelming inequalities and concentrations revealed by official Inland Revenue statistics and surveys, and by various studies based upon these. We assess the degree to which a fairer distribution has emerged over the past two decades and conclude that no such equalising tendency can be identified when necessary adjustments and qualifications are made to the official data.

As far as *income* is concerned, we feel that the basis of income unit for Inland Revenue statistics can be influenced by various changes over time and that it does not fit other data sources. We are aware of sources of income not covered by the official data, and that lifetime earnings patterns cannot be revealed by "snapshot" pictures. We seriously doubt whether any redistribution which has occurred has benefited those at the bottom end of the distribution. Finally we are alarmed that the discontinuing of the adjusted CSO figures was not accompanied by provision of any new analysis.

On *wealth* we have similar reservations: there are many people and many forms of wealth not covered by the official figures, and the basis of inference through mortality multipliers is suspect. We consider both the overall distribution of wealth, and the concentration of holdings of particular forms of wealth, such as shares and household goods. (The former is also of relevance to the Reference on Income from Companies.) We are particularly concerned that half the population have no dutiable wealth, and a similar proportion derive no benefit from home ownership. When these are taken into account we can find no evidence of any trend towards a fairer distribution of wealth.

We are particularly concerned that wealth carries with it power and control as well as financial benefit, particularly with share ownership, and that the concept of income as "command over economic resources" proposed by the Minority Report of the Royal Commission on Taxation has not been absorbed into our taxation principles. Finally we stress the relationship between taxation of wealth and adequate data on wealth with particular reference to the proposed Capital Transfer Tax.

In *Section 2: Changing Tax Burdens* we look in more detail at the distribution of incomes *after* tax, and show that the burden has decreased at the top end. It is clear that the direction of changes (towards or away from progressivenesss) has altered over the post-war period, and that there is a correlation with whether a Labour or Conservative government is in office.

Using an assumption of a stable distribution of income as the basis for our methodological approach, we show how the general tendency has been for tax liability to increase disproportionately upon lower incomes and families with children. Within the period under consideration (1954/5 to 1974/5) there is evidence that progressiveness was compromised by Conservative administrations particularly. We also conclude that the current Government has a considerable way to go if the intention is to reverse this tendency between 1970 and 1974.

We look at national insurance contributions, which we find to be regressive in their impact for a number of reasons. Finally we draw attention to investment as opposed to earned income, and offer some conclusions, implications and proposals with respect to future taxation policy; particular attention is given to the desirability of reduced rates of taxation, the possibly over-wide range of income covered by the standard rate, and the levels of tax thresholds.

*Section Three: Directors' Pay, Other High Incomes and Benefits* is also of relevance to the other two references currently before the Royal Commission. We offer four company case studies in order to identify the kind of remuneration (both salary and non-salary) involved, and the kind of differentials provided against the employed workforce. We move on to directors' remuneration more generally and question the basis for directorships (and the efficiency of directors) as well as the amount of benefit to them over and above basic salaries. In this context we are again concerned at power and control dimensions, particularly with respect to multiple directorships.

We then turn to the very wide range of fringe benefits which are quite disproportionately available to the upper echelons of the corporate hierarchy. Such benefits have been increasing in significance, and include cars, housing, holidays, expenses, health care, pensions, share options and bonus schemes. All reduce the tax liability which would be incurred by their cash equivalents, and as such equate to very high amounts of gross pay at higher marginal rates of taxation. Companies acknowledge that such benefits represent twice the proportion of pay costs at higher employee levels than overall, and our estimate is that their combined post-tax value to the recipient can be in the order of £4,400 per annum. The gross salary equivalent – and the consequent "loss" to the Inland Revenue – are therefore very substantial indeed, and there is a strong case for making such fringe benefits taxable.

Finally we are struck by the disturbing contrast between the generous attitude of companies towards fringe benefits for directors and senior executives and their resistance, which we have of course experienced in a collective bargaining context, to similar but comparatively modest claims for enhanced provisions for employees (e.g. holidays and pensions). (N.B. One particular benefit, scrip issues, is dealt with in detail in Section 4 of our Evidence on Income from Companies.)

In *Section 4: Some Wider Considerations*, we look critically at sources of and further needs for information beyond what is provided by Inland Revenue statistics. We draw attention to the limitations of key official data (the New Earnings Survey, wage rates indices, the Family Expenditure Survey and the Retail Price Index) having relevance to this Standing Reference. We also argue the need for official data on trends in real disposable income (taking account of direct taxes, price changes and means-tested benefits) for different income levels and different family composition. Finally we offer a critical review of the annual *Economic Trends* articles on the Incidence of Taxation and Benefits, drawing those conclusions sustainable within the limitations of the methodology and definitions.

*Section Five: Some Further Proposals for the Future* suggests modifications and new developments in the collection, presentation and analysis of official data which could bring about a significant increase in our general ability to discern trends in the distributions of income and wealth. Particular attention is given to effective as opposed to nominal tax rates; to accounting periods longer than a year; to the construction of anonymous profiles; and to the possibilities of linking data from various sources (the Inland Revenue, the Family Expenditure Survey and the New Earnings Survey, the Population Census and Social Security data offers a wide range of possibilities). Finally the case is argued for the inclusion of an income question in the Population Census, a measure which has opened new possibilities of analysis and understanding in the USA.

An *Appendix* to our Evidence has again been added in the form of a Trade Union Research Unit Technical Note: *Equal Pay: A Critical Review of Progress* offers an up-to-date and detailed study of what we feel to be a key aspect of income distribution.

# 1

# The Existing Evidence

On the basis of existing published evidence it is not possible to say with certainty whether inequality of income and wealth is decreasing. In this Section, therefore, we concentrate on dispelling misconceptions and indicating some of the main problems with the data. Since much has already been written on this subject we do not try to be comprehensive; rather we aim to pinpoint aspects that will be taken up further in Section 2. Before turning to the evidence, however, it may be helpful if we briefly outline the conceptual issues. The framework of any discussion will in this way be more readily at hand.

*Conceptual Issues*

Much of the public debate has generated heat rather than light and one reason for this has been the failure to distinguish separate subjects. At the outset, therefore, it may be useful to isolate two different meanings of the phrase "trends in the size distribution of income". Firstly, there is the subject of the absolute level of income for different people at different dates, and hence in aggregate the rate of growth of total personal income. This question undoubtedly has important bearing on what in effect happens to the "share out" and any comprehensive discussion of the consequences of alternative distribution arrangements would need to take account of this aspect. Secondly there is the question, what is the share of total personal income in fact held by different groups at different times? It is the statistical measurement of this aspect which is our prime concern in this section, and in fact this second question taken alone has itself been the subject of much controversy.

To some extent the difficulty in getting consensus on the direction of past trends or the magnitudes involved stems from the fact that the question which is being asked is one to which there can be no single answer. Lampman succinctly yet forcibly brought this point out when addressing the American Economic Association in 1967:

> "there is no single size distribution of income by observation of which one can definitely establish whether 'economic inequality' has increased or decreased. Any particular representation of the income distribution yields a picture of income inequality which is determined to a significant degree by the selection of definitions of income, income receiving unit, and income period, as well as the basis for ranking and the methods of summarising the data. Hence any single ranking presented as a definitive statement of 'the facts' is best regarded as an illusory treatment of an elusive reality."
>
> Lampman, R.J. *American Economic Association, Papers and Proceedings, 1967*

There is little hope for comfort therefore for the person who seeks a single answer to the question "Are incomes becoming more equal?" or "Given present institutional arrangements will incomes become less unequal in the future?". And even with much better sources of data the above aspects of the problem would still remain. Nevertheless, the existing data is in fact still far from adequate and it is on the question of the sources of information that we want to concentrate.

*Inland Revenue Data on Income Distribution*

The Inland Revenue Surveys of Personal Incomes are a main source of evidence on income distribution in Britain and it is with these that we will begin. One reason why this source is inevitably the one used as the basis in any discussion of trends is that a survey of a relatively similar type has here been carried out continually for several decades and that on each occasion the coverage of the survey is sufficiently similar for many people to feel that one is comparing like with like. In fact only the Inland Revenue Surveys can claim to be even potentially useful for the entire post-war period. Most of the authors on this subject have however adjusted the "raw" data in various ways and given varying weight to its deficiencies and it is on the adequacy or otherwise of what has been done in this respect that we will comment.

The scope of the Inland Revenue Surveys of Personal Incomes is as follows: firstly, they are concerned with income as defined for tax purposes. Incomes below the effective exemption limits and all types of non-taxable income above these limits are therefore excluded. The definition of income adopted therefore falls far short of including all additions to purchasing power and for this reason is far from ideal for our purpose. Secondly, the unit is as defined for tax purposes. This means that a married couple with or without children is simply counted as one unit, as are single persons. The definition of the unit therefore does not conform to either the individual, the family or the household. Moreover, there is no attempt to adjust the unit to a per capita basis and in this way take account of the different needs of families of different sizes. It is clear, therefore, that there are serious deficiencies for our purpose with the Inland Revenue Survey of Personal Incomes "raw" data, and that anyone would do well to use it merely as a backcloth against which to isolate the relative importance of different omitted factors with respect to conclusions about trends in the distribution of income over time. Nevertheless, the Inland Revenue itself sometimes comments on the trends as revealed by the "raw" data which it publishes. And it is instructive to consider what they say.

After the publication of the 1948/9 results the Inland Revenue claimed that there had been a marked reduction in inequality since the previous survey of 1938/9. It was with the objective of disputing the validity of this conclusion that Titmuss wrote his now famous critique of the Inland Revenue Statistics *Income Distribution and Social Change.* Our immediate concern here however is with trends in the post-war period. The Inland Revenue also has recently had something to say about these. In 1972 it prefaced the results of the 1969/70 Survey with a historical review which concluded "In short, the broad picture of the last twenty years is of a tendency for variations between incomes to diminish". The main basis for the Inland Revenue conclusion is the movement of the "Pareto Index" over the period. This is not the place to go into the details of the construction of the index but it suffices to say that the higher its value the less is the 'official' interpretation of inequality. In fact the Pareto Index was 1.95 in 1949/50 and 2.55 in 1969/70.

In order to see in slightly more detail what has in fact happened we constructed estimates of the respective shares of different inter-percentile groups for 1949/50 and 1969/70. These estimates are presented in Table 1.

**TABLE 1**
**PERCENTAGE DISTRIBUTION OF INCOMES BEFORE TAX**

| | *Top 1%* | *Top 5%* | *Top 10%* | *Top 30%* | *Top 40%* | *Bottom 30%* |
|---|---|---|---|---|---|---|
| 1949/50 | 10.5 | 22.9 | 31.0 | 53.1 | 61.5 | 14.2 |
| 1969/70 | 6.7 | 15.5 | 25.5 | 52.0 | 62.4 | 13.2 |

From Table 1 it can be seen that the top 30% receive over 3½ times as much of the total than that received by the bottom 30%. And this was as true in 1969/70 as it was in 1949/50. Discussion of changes over time should be seen in the context of the extent of inequality in the existing structure. From Table 1 it can also be seen that over the post-war period the top 40% actually improved their position and at the same time the bottom 30% lost ground. Any attempt to summarise changes in the distribution by means of a single measure of inequality are therefore likely, as pointed out by Lampman in the quote in our introduction, to give a misleading impression of unambiguous movements in a situation where no such conclusions are valid. In fact what has happened in the above instance is that the Pareto Index is based solely on what is happening in the upper ranges of income (and in only a very approximate fashion there) and it therefore does not capture the considerable decline in the share of total income received by lower income ranges. The first important conclusion of this section is therefore that even if for our purposes there were no deficiencies in the Inland Revenue data, there is still no unambiguous evidence of a clear trend towards greater equality of income, and many people on looking at the evidence would claim that inequality had increased.

*The Central Statistical Office Estimates of Income Distribution*

For the post-war period up until 1967 the CSO produced estimates of the distribution of personal income. These tables were included in the Blue Book *National Income and Expenditure.* The first difference between these estimates and the "raw" returns considered above was that the CSO estimates were on a calendar year basis whereas the Inland Revenue returns were for the financial year. The CSO estimates could therefore be more easily compared with other items in the National Income Accounts. The derivation of the CSO estimates was as follows: they were the result of adjusting the IR estimates to include, among other things, incomes below the effective exemption limit down to persons receiving not less than £50 a year, and the inclusion of supplementary benefits and other national insurance benefits which are not liable to tax (unemployment, sickness, maternity, injury and disablement benefit etc.). Estimates for each item were attributed to what seemed to be the most appropriate income ranges. It was the CSO estimates which formed the basis of much of the "unofficial" work on trends in income distribution over time e.g. Nicholson for the period 1949-63. It is therefore right that we should regard the absence of the CSO estimates for the post-1967 period as a great loss for our purposes. The official justification for discontinuing them "because of the increasing amount of estimation required" would have carried more weight if something superior had been substituted. In effect we are now left to rely on the far less satisfactory "raw" returns.

In Table 2 we present Nicholson's tabulation of the CSO estimates for the period 1949-63.

TABLE 2
PERCENTAGE DISTRIBUTION OF INCOME BEFORE TAX

| | *Top 1%* | *Top 5%* | *Top 10%* | *Top 40%* | *Bottom 30%* |
|---|---|---|---|---|---|
| 1949 | 11.2 | 23.8 | 33.2 | 68.1 | 12.7 |
| 1957 | 8.2 | 19.1 | 28.1 | 65.7 | 11.3 |
| 1959 | 8.4 | 19.9 | 29.4 | 67.8 | 9.7 |
| 1963 | 7.9 | 19.1 | 28.7 | 67.7 | 9.7 |

On the basis of this Table Nicholson concluded that "this trend (towards a reduction in the degree of inequality) continued to about the middle of the 1950s; that since 1957 the movement towards equality has ceased". Let us examine each of these two conclusion in turn. Firstly, the trend towards increased equality up until 1957 is by no means unambiguous (although Nicholson does recognise this by saying that too much reliability cannot be placed on the movements of the bottom income ranges). Secondly, it is clear that the trend has not been towards equality in the 1957-1963 period (even the Pareto index applied to the 1957 and 1963 figures is unlikely to have shown a move towards equality).

Atkinson, writing in *Wealth, Income and Inequality* updated the Nicholson estimates for the period until 1967. The 1963 and 1967 estimates are shown in Table 3.

TABLE 3
PERCENTAGE DISTRIBUTION OF INCOMES BEFORE TAX

| | *Top 1%* | *Top 5%* | *Top 10%* | *Top 40%* | *Bottom 30%* |
|---|---|---|---|---|---|
| 1963 | 7.9 | 19.1 | 28.7 | 67.7 | 9.7 |
| 1967 | 7.4 | 18.4 | 28.0 | 66.9 | 10.4 |

Atkinson concludes that "the extension of the period to 1967 does not affect Nicholson's conclusions that 'the most considerable change is that which took place between 1949 and 1957' ". Overall however (1949-67) it does appear that the redistribution which did occur was from the top to the near the top income ranges. These figures do not provide much comfort for those in the lower and middle income ranges. In fact the CSO estimates show a deterioration in the position of the top 40% over the period 1949-67 whereas the "raw" returns showed an improvement for this group over a closely similar period.

### *Deficiencies with the Official Data on Incomes*

There are undoubtedly serious deficiencies in the basic IR and CSO data for estimating the distribution of income at a point in time and we will return to this issue shortly. First, however, it remains to be shown that these significant deficiencies do not cease to be important when trends over time are being considered. It might at first sight appear surprising that such claims should ever have been made, but if the missing sources of income could be shown to maintain the same relationship to the recorded income in successive years then it would clearly be easier to measure trends than distributions at one point in time. Nicholson, for example, is one person who clearly does think that the deficiencies do "net out" when considering trends in the post-war period. Referring to the CSO figures he says that we do "have a consistently defined aggregate . . . and one which is adequate for picking out changing trends in the distribution of income in post-war years". And he claimed that much of Titmuss's criticism was directed at the difficulties involved in comparing the pre- and post-war periods (as attempted by Lydall). In particular he points out that the 1938 tabulations relate to the incomes of only some 3 million income recipients, whereas the post-war distribution relates to 26 million incomes. But that between 1949 and 1963 the increase was only 1.2 million units. Such an increase "has not been sufficiently great to invalidate the later comparisons" he claims.

Nicholson in referring to the number of units has however only referred to one aspect of the problem and his conclusions do not appear to remain valid when several other important aspects are taken into account. For example, the omitted sources of income include items such as capital gains, the imputed rent on owner-occupied houses, fringe benefits, and pension contributions. With respect to these items Atkinson's conclusion that "there are good grounds for expecting that the relative importance of 'missing' income increased during the post-war period" seems nearer the mark, and we are inclined to agree with him when he says "it is quite possible therefore that the income tax distribution may provide a misleading impression of the trends in income distribution". Much more research is required before a comprehensive answer can be given but a few illustrative examples are sufficient to make the general point.

One of the most serious omissions is undoubtedly capital gains. Unrealised capital gains clearly represent an addition to the individual's command over the use of scarce resources. He can for example use them as collateral as a basis for borrowing money. Prest and Stark estimated from information on asset-holding the capital gains accruing in 1959 and allocated these to different income ranges. Their analysis showed that capital gains accrue largely to people in the upper income ranges.* Therefore an increase in capital gains over the post-war period as a whole would

*The share of the top 1 per cent of income rises from 8 to 14 per cent and the share of the top five per cent from 19 to 27 per cent.

give rise to a greater degree of trend inequality than is reflected in the IR/CSO data.

Another aspect of the deficiencies with the official data is, as noted earlier, that the IR/CSO estimates relate to income of units of varying sizes from single persons to large families. Prest and Stark "try to compare the distribution of income over time in such a way that we abstract from the effect of the changing size of income units". On this basis the degree of inequality is seen to be slightly less and the bottom 30% of the distribution increases its share of the total from 10% in 1949 to 14% in 1967 (all the previous estimates showed a decline for this group over the period as a whole). Adjustment to take account of the needs of income units of different sizes is therefore undoubtedly important for interpreting trends over time, but this is not the only type of structural change which is important. Other important factors are changes in marriage patterns, changes in the age structure of the population, and changes in the level of unemployment. Prest and Stark, for example, found that the ageing of the population, in particular the increase in the number of pensioners, affected the trends observed in the post-war period.

A final and even more formidable deficiency with the official data which needs to be considered but which has not yet been mentioned is whether annual "snapshot" pictures can ever truly reflect the prevailing income distribution. There are in fact two problems to be disentangled. Firstly, the extent to which increased prosperity in general has been shared between different generations. And secondly, the systematic variation of income with different stages of the lifecycle of an individual. In either case the way to answer the question is to collect data on the lifetime income of individuals.

*Evidence on the Distribution of Personal Wealth*

This part comments briefly on the trends in the distribution of wealth in Britain in the 1960s. One reason why it is much shorter than that on income is because many of the issues raised in that discussion also apply to wealth. For example, the need to look at changes in the structure of society and the lifecycle factors. It is important to stress, however, that the relative length of the parts is in no way intended to reflect the relative importance of the subjects. In fact there is a particularly urgent need for "official" investigations into changes in the distribution of wealth over time and the effect of particular tax measures on this.

The main source of information both for the "official" and the "adjusted" estimates is the Estate Duty returns. Part of Atkinson and Harrison's work involves the adjusting of the "raw" Estate Duty data so as to take account of its most obvious deficiencies. They would however be the first to agree that even at their best the Estate Duty returns represent only an indirect source of evidence, the assumption having to be made throughout that evidence on deaths occurring in any one year can be adjusted so that they represent a random sample of the living. This method is obviously far from ideal. A far more accurate way to measure the distribution of wealth is by means of a compulsory wealth census of the living. But there was no such census during the 1960s in Britain.

The official Inland Revenue series of estimates was first constructed for 1960 and there have been annual estimates ever since. The series is reproduced for the Top 1%, 5% and 10% in Table 4. The first striking feature that can be seen from the Table is that 90% of the adult population owned less than half the total wealth throughout the period (in fact, 50% of the population possessed less than 10% of it). With respect to the top 10%, however, the picture as presented by the official statistics does give the impression that inequality is decreasing.*

**TABLE 4**
**DISTRIBUTION OF WEALTH – IR ESTIMATES 1960-71**

| *Year* | *Share of total wealth held by top % of wealth holders* | | |
|---|---|---|---|
| | *1%* | *5%* | *10%* |
| 1960 | 28.3 | 50.9 | 63.0 |
| 1961 | 28.0 | 50.6 | 62.5 |
| 1962 | 27.1 | 48.8 | 60.6 |
| 1963 | 26.6 | 49.9 | 62.0 |
| 1964 | 25.8 | 48.4 | 60.3 |
| 1965 | 24.3 | 46.3 | 58.3 |
| 1966 | 22.7 | 43.6 | 55.8 |
| 1967 | 22.8 | 43.6 | 55.5 |
| 1968 | 23.7 | 45.2 | 57.1 |
| 1969 | 21.3 | 41.2 | 52.8 |
| 1970 | 20.7 | 40.9 | 51.9 |
| 1971 | 20.4 | 40.1 | 51.6 |

*The Adjustments needed to the Wealth Data*

One important finding of the research of Atkinson and Harrison is that the "official" estimates considerably overestimate the trend towards less inequality with respect to the fortunes of the top 10%. Four of the main types of adjustment which are made to the "official" series concern missing people, missing wealth, the choice of mortality multipliers, and

*Although the Gini coefficient of concentration rose from 64% to 66% between 1971 and 1972 for this distribution.

the effects of short-term movements in share prices. Here we will just briefly look at each in turn.

Firstly, concerning missing people. In 1969 the "official" figures were based on 280,000 estates. There were, however, 620,000 "adult" deaths that year. About half of the total estates were therefore outside the compass of the estimates. As a result the total number of wealth holders shown in the official statistics in any year were considerably less than the total adult population. In 1971 there were 18.6 million "estimated" wealth holders, but an adult population of some 39 million. Atkinson and Harrison show that taking account of these completely ignored people not only increases the degree of concentration of wealth but also causes the trend towards greater equality to be considerably less marked.

This approach is confirmed by the Gini coefficients of concentration presented by the Inland Revenue. Their series A reflects the wealth owners' distribution, whilst series B is adjusted to take account of the whole of the population aged 15 and over assuming that those not included in Series A have no wealth at all:

**TABLE 5**
**GINI PERCENTAGES**

| | *1962* | *1963* | *1964* | *1965* | *1966* | *1967* | *1968* | *1969* | *1970* | *1971* | *1972* |
|---|---|---|---|---|---|---|---|---|---|---|---|
| Series A | 72 | 73 | 72 | 70 | 67 | 67 | 68 | 65 | 65 | 64 | 66 |
| Series B | 87 | 87 | 86 | 86 | 86 | 86 | 87 | 85 | 85 | 84 | 86 |

Secondly we turn to important categories of personal wealth which are missing from the Estate Duty statistics. Pensions, which disappear on death, are one example. Some settled property, which is exempt from death duties, is another. Titmuss has of course drawn attention to a whole range of arrangements which enable estate duty to be avoided and/or estimates of income and wealth concentration to be understated. These include gifts, covenants, family settlements, discretionary trusts, life assurance, incorporation and arrangements abroad. He also raises the question of undistributed profits, considered in Sections 2 and 3 of the TGWU Evidence on Company Income. Thirdly there is the fact that mortality rates vary with social class. The Inland Revenue recognises this and does choose more than one "blow-up" multiplier in attempt to capture this effect. The accuracy with which they do so is, however, a matter of dispute. Also disputed is the way they take account of changes in trends in mortality rates over time. Finally there is the fact that "As a short term effect changes in the relative prices of fixed-interest securities and ordinary shares can also make noticeable differences in the degree of concentration from one year to another". (Revell.) This is so because the composition of portfolios is different, in general, for the top wealth holders compared to those with little wealth (attention to the forms of wealth holding was given in TGWU Evidence on Company Income, Section 2; a more detailed picture is presented in the tables at the end of this Section). It is clearly important, therefore, to interpret the trends in the distribution of wealth in the light of movements in share prices and to compare "peak" with "peak" or "trough" with "trough".

Adjustments of the above type are clearly of importance for purposes of examining trends over time with respect to the share of total wealth held by the top 10%. And it is the well-being of this top 10% which has attracted almost all of the attention in the continuing debate (public and academic). However, even though we know very little about the bottom 90% this part would not be complete without at least a few remarks concerning their changing fortunes. In the future it is important that the overall wealth distribution is brought fully into the limelight. In particular the "causes" of any increase which has occurred in the shares of "the rest" must be examined carefully. Alan Day, for example, hits on one obvious fact when he says that the increases gained by "the rest" are "largely to be attributed to the spread of owner-occupation and to the rapid rise in house prices". What he doesn't say is the equally obvious corollary that these improvements will have been of no comfort to that half of the total households in Britain who do not own their own homes: and in fact it may well have made things worse for them. This is, however, only a specific point. In general terms the important fact is that there is clearly a need to know to where the wealth is going as well as where it is coming from. As far as one can tell there may have been a gradual "trickling down" of wealth in Britain in the 1960s but the transfer appears to be from the very rich to the rich and perhaps to the less rich. There is certainly no evidence that it has been from the rich to the poor.

*Some Implications*

There can be no doubt that excessive inequalities exist in the distributions of income and – more particularly – wealth in post-war Britain. Moreover, there are grounds for believing that the official presentation of data on these distributions is both understating the degree of concentration and overstating the tendencies towards more equality.

The derivation of our knowledge of these areas from Inland Revenue data is necessarily governed by the principles and comprehensiveness of taxation provisions, together with the abilities of people to arrange their receipts and holdings in such ways as to avoid or minimise tax liability. The importance that this places upon future taxation reforms and developments is crucial, for more reliable and comprehensive data will be both a precondition and a by-product of more effective wealth taxation (we have in mind here the capital transfer tax). It is to be hoped that the Royal Commission will give particular attention to this consideration, as well as to the underlying concept of Income which should govern tax liability. As we argued in our Evidence on Company Income the definition adopted by the Minority Report of the Royal Commission on Taxation, of "command over economic resources" is of key relevance, reflecting as it does both the economic and control elements of wealth ownership alongside conventional income.

**TABLE 6**
**PERCENTAGE OF EACH TYPE OF HOLDING HELD BY GROUPS IN 1971**

| *Total net value of estate* | | *over* | *under* |
|---|---|---|---|
| *Type of holding* | | *£10,000* % | *£10,000* % |
| 1 | National Svng Certs & Prem. Bonds | 39 | 61 |
| 2 | Brit. Gov. Bonds | 51.7 | 48.3 |
| 3 – 6 | Other Gov. Securities | 87 | 13 |
| 7 – 10 | Municipal, foreign & c'wealth securities | 88.4 | 11.6 |
| 11 | GB unquoted Ord. shares | 94.5 | 5.5 |
| 12 | " Pref. & debentures etc. | 96.5 | 3.5 |
| 13 | GB quoted Inv. Trust Ord. shares | 95.75 | 4.25 |
| 14 | " Ord. shares | 94.8 | 5.2 |
| 15 | " Pref. debentures etc. | 90.5 | 9.5 |
| 16 – 18 | Foreign unquoted stocks | 96.9 | 3.1 |
| 19 | Unit trusts | 70.8 | 29.2 |
| 3 – 19 | All stocks and shares | 92.7 | 7.3 |
| 20/22/23 | Money on mortgage and on bonds and securities | 65.2 | 34.8 |
| 21 | Shares and deposits in Bldg. Socs. | 55.9 | 44.1 |
| 25 | H'hold goods, pictures, china etc. | 36.7 | 63.3 |
| 26 | Life assurance policies | 32.5 | 67.5 |
| 27 | Cash in the house | 30.6 | 69.4 |
| 28 | " Nat. & Trustee Svgs. Bank | 19.5 | 80.5 |
| 29 | " Deposit accounts | 53.6 | 46.4 |
| 30 | " Current accounts | 48.2 | 51.8 |
| 30A | Cash gifts | 87.2 | 12.9 |
| 31 – 7 | Trade, business & other assets | 66 | 34 |
| 24/39/41 | Other personalty | 48.4 | 51.6 |
| 48 | Net Personal Wealth | 58 | 42 |
| 49/50 | Land | 95.3 | 4.8 |
| 51/53 | Residential Buildings | 37.1 | 62.9 |

**TABLE 6 CONTINUED**

| *Type of holding* | | *over £10,000* % | *under £10,000* % |
|---|---|---|---|
| 52/54–7 | Other property | 76.7 | 23.3 |
| 62 | Net landed property | 47.2 | 52.8 |
| | | 54.9 | 45.1 |

*Source: Inland Revenue Statistics for year 1970-71,* Table 94 (Code numbers are those used by the I.R.)

It is interesting to look in more detail at the distributions of shareholdings – which reflect industrial and financial control as well as economic resources – and of household goods. The latter appear to be more evenly distributed from the evidence in Table 6 (which is what one might expect) but Table 8 shows this to be far from the case.

**TABLE 7**
**DISTRIBUTION OF SHAREHOLDINGS (3 – 19) 1971 TO THOSE HAVING TOTAL NET WEALTH OF:**

| *range of net wealth* | *percentage held* | *cumulative* % |
|---|---|---|
| £200,000 or more | 21.4 | 21.4 |
| £100,000 – £200,000 | 17.1 | 38.5 |
| £50,000 – £100,000 | 22.8 | 61.3 |
| £20,000 – £50,000 | 22.7 | 84 |
| £15,000 – £20,000 | 4.5 | 88.5 |
| £10,000 – £15,000 | 4.3 | 92.8 |
| £5,000 – £10,000 | 4.4 | 97.2 |
| £3,000 – £5,000 | 1.3 | 98.5 |
| £1,000 – £3,000 | 1.1 | 99.6 |
| Less than £1,000 | 0.3 | 99.9 |

*Source:* As Table 6

**TABLE 8**
**DISTRIBUTION OF 'HOUSEHOLD GOODS' (25) 1971**

| *range of net wealth held* | *per capita holding* £ | |
|---|---|---|
| Less than £1,000 | 100 ) | |
| £1,000 – £3,000 | 185 – ) | |
| £3,000 – £5,000 | 230 – ) | |
| £5,000 – £10,000 | 315 – ) | cumulatively 85.7% of those with holdings of this type. |

**TABLE 8 CONTINUED**

| *range of net wealth held* | *per capita holding* | |
|---|---|---|
| £ 10,000 – £15,000 | 392 | |
| £ 15,000 – £20,000 | 428 | |
| £ 20,000 – £50,000 | 693 | |
| £ 50,000 – £100,000 | 1480 | |
| £100,000 – £200,000 | 2700 | |
| over £200,000 | 10800 | (or one hundred times that held by the least wealthy) |

*Source:* As Table 6

References:


Atkinson, A.B. *Unequal Shares: wealth in Britain*, Allen Lane 1972.

Atkinson, A.B. (Ed.) *Wealth, Income and Inequality*, Penguin Modern Economic Readings 1973. Includes the article Nicholson, R.J. "The Distribution of Personal Income".

Atkinson, A.B. and Harrison A.J. *The Distribution of Wealth in Britain*, forthcoming Cambridge University Press.

Lampman, R.J. "The Effectiveness of some institutions in changing the distribution of income" American Economic Association, *Papers and Proceedings 1967.*

Lydall, H.F. "The Long Term Trend in the Size Distribution of Income" *Journal of the Royal Statistical Society*, Series A 1959.

Prest, A.R. and Stark, T. "Some Aspects of the Distribution of Income Since World War II" Manchester School 1967.

Revell, J. "Changes in the Social Distribution of Property in Britain during the 20th Century" *Third International Conference of Economic History 1965.*

Titmuss, R.M. *Income Distribution and Social Change*, Allen and Unwin, 1962.

Day, A. "Wealth/Who owns it?", *The Observer*, 20 January 1974.

# 2

# Changing Tax Burden

## Introduction

Income Tax and surtax are one of the main methods by which the distribution of income can be altered. Indeed, the tax system is designed to take larger slices of income from those with the highest earnings. Thus, in the tax year 1974/5, excluding the effect of allowances, rates of taxation ranged from 33 per cent on taxable incomes up to £4,500 per year, to 83 per cent at £20,000 and over. Clearly the intended effect of income tax and surtax is to reduce the degree of inequality of before-tax incomes. Because direct taxes reduce the degree of inequality of incomes they are called "progressive". However, this degree of progressiveness can change over the years, and it is these changes which will be examined in this section. Also, some account will be taken of the impact of national insurance contributions, both flat rate and graduated, upon the distribution of income.

### *Effect of Tax on the Personal Distribution of Income*

In Section 1 the before-tax distribution of income was examined both on the basis of the raw Inland Revenue data and on the CSO adjusted information. Table 1 below presents an updated version of R.J. Nicholson's data on the proportion of after-tax income of various groups of income recipients.

**TABLE 1**
**PERCENTAGE OF INCOME RECEIVED AFTER TAX IN 1949, 1957, 1963 and 1967**

| *Group of income recipients* | *1949* | *1957* | *1963* | *1967* |
|---|---|---|---|---|
| Top 1% | 6.4 | 5.0 | 5.2 | 4.9 |
| 2 – 5% | 11.3 | 9.9 | 10.5 | 9.9 |
| 6 10% | 9.4 | 9.1 | 9.5 | 9.5 |
| 11 – 40% | 37.0 | 38.5 | 39.5 | 39.2 |
| 41 – 70% | 21.3 | 24.0 | 23.5 | 24.5 |
| Bottom 30% | 14.6 | 13.4 | 11.8 | 12.0 |

*Source:* Nicholson *op.cit.*

Table 1, while similar to the before-tax distribution, infers that the reduction in the proportion of income received after tax by the top 5% between 1949 and 1957 was not of the same order of magnitude. The middle-income groups gained, although not uniformly, while there has been a deterioration for the bottom 30%.

An illustration of the way in which the tax burden has decreased at the top end of the income distribution is given in Table 2:

**TABLE 2**
**AFTER TAX INCOME AS A PERCENTAGE OF BEFORE TAX INCOME**

| *Group of recipients* | *1949/50* | *1959/60* | *1964/65* | *1970/71* | *1971/72* |
|---|---|---|---|---|---|
| top 50 thousand | 36 | 42 | 43 | 40 | 45 |
| second 50 thousand | 57 | 61 | 63 | 56 | 60 |
| next 100 thousand | 65 | 68 | 69 | 63 | 66 |
| next 300 thousand | 71 | 76 | 75 | 68 | 73 |

*Source:* Inland Revenue Statistics

The information in Table 2 is based upon the raw Inland Revenue data and is not strictly comparable with that in Table 1. However, it is apparent that between 1949/50 and 1959/60 there were significant increases in the proportion of income that was retained by the top income recipients. Over the period 1964/5 to 1970/71 there has been a slight decline in the proportion of income kept by the top 50 thousand income recipients, while for the groups below this there was a return to the 1949/50 position or worse. Since 1970/71 the position has again changed, the top income groups retaining even greater proportions of their incomes after tax. Judging by the timing of changes in the trends displayed in Table 2, it is probable that a major influence has been the political party which was in office. Conservative governments tend to lessen the burden of taxation on the top end of the income distribution, while Labour governments have increased it.

It is clear that the degree of progressiveness of the income tax system is not a fixed parameter. There has been a tendency to lower the tax burden at the top end of the income distribution while increasing it at the bottom. Atkinson's conclusion that the available data indicates the rich lost ground, but so did the poor, should be seen in the context of a tax system that has become less progressive, partially offsetting any moves towards greater equality of incomes.

The reservations expressed in Section 1 about the adequacy of data on the distribution of income also apply to the figures presented here, particularly with respect to the lack of information about what has been happening at the bottom end of the distribution. A partial analysis of the impact of direct taxation upon earned incomes can be constructed by the use of specific assumptions about the shape of the distribution; this we undertake below.

### *Income Tax and a Stable Distribution of Income*

The available evidence on the dispersion of employment incomes indicates that over nearly 90 years there has been little change in the shape of the earnings distribution. This is illustrated in Table 3 which shows that as a percentage of median weekly earnings the lowest decile was 68.6 in 1886 and in 1974; at the highest decile the percentages were 143.1 in 1886, and 144.1 in 1974. While there are minor changes in the relative position of the lowest and highest deciles between different years the general picture is one of remarkable stability.*

**TABLE 3**
**DISPERSION OF WEEKLY EARNINGS, MANUAL WORKER 1886-1974**

| *Year* | *Lowest decile* | *Lower quartile* | *Median* | *Upper quartile* | *Highest decile* |
|---|---|---|---|---|---|
| 1886 | 68.6 | 82.8 | 100.0 | 121.7 | 143.1 |
| 1938 | 67.7 | 82.1 | 100.0 | 118.5 | 139.9 |
| 1960 | 70.6 | 82.6 | 100.0 | 121.7 | 145.2 |
| 1965 | 69.7 | 82.9 | 100.0 | 121.4 | 143.9 |
| 1970 | 67.3 | 81.1 | 100.0 | 122.3 | 147.2 |
| 1973 | 67.3 | 81.4 | 100.0 | 121.6 | 145.3 |
| 1974 | 68.6 | 82.2 | 100.0 | 121.0 | 144.1 |

Bodies such as the NBPI (*Report No. 169*, "General Problems of Low Pay") and various academics have been struck by the seemingly immutable nature of the distribution of earned incomes. The latter seek to explain the phenomenon by a range of overlapping and, at times, conflicting theories. Some prefer stochastic theories which give the operation of the rules of chance a predominant role, while others turn to the part played by institutional and social factors. Without taking any set position on the underlying causes which have resulted in a relatively stable dispersion of earned incomes, it is possible to use the observed state of affairs to assess the impact of various government policies.

Indeed it would seem imperative to have a model of the distribution of income against which to assess the redistributive impact of government policies. Thus, while the distribution of income may not be absolutely rigid, an assumption that it is will give a broad outline of the putative impact of various government policies. In particular the impact

---

*Unfortunately the data in Table 3 only refer to manual workers. However, there is no evidence to suggest any significant departure from this pattern for non-manual workers.

of the two major direct deductions from gross earnings (income tax and national insurance) can be assessed.

While the shape of the before-tax distribution of earned income may remain reasonably static, it does not necessarily follow that the after-tax distribution does likewise. The main reasons why the after-tax distribution is partially independent of the before-tax distribution are the impact of inflation and changes in tax rates. The former gives rise to a phenomenon called "fiscal drag" whereby maintaining a constant relationship with the distribution of earned income will, if tax rates do not change, result in the deduction of increasing amounts of tax. Changes in tax rates, often presented as offsetting "fiscal drag", can be designed to have a differential impact on various income levels. In view of this it is instructive to examine how the tax burden has changed over the past twenty years.

In the Tables and Figures that follow it has been assumed that while the dispersion of incomes is stable incomes have increased in line with the Department of Employment's annual October earnings enquiry. The dispersion around average earnings is consistent with the actual spread of earned incomes. Two-thirds of average earnings corresponds closely with the NBPI's definition of low pay (Report No. 169) and is often used in academic studies of low pay – twenty times average earnings (£42,557 per annum in 1973/74) is in line with the salaries of high-paid company executives.

Figures 1 and 2 illustrate changes in the tax burden at the bottom end of the earnings distribution over the past twenty years. Figure 1 shows income tax as a percentage of total earnings for workers who maintained their same relative position in the earnings distribution 1954/5 to 1974/5. The low-paid worker is assumed to be one who earned two-thirds of national average earnings each year and the higher-paid worker one with one-and-a-half times the average. In Figure 1 all workers are assumed to be single person households, but the way in which families of different sizes were affected is shown in Figure 2.

Figures 1 and 2 clearly show that as a percentage of gross earnings the additional burdens of income taxation were levied disproportionately onto the low-paid and families with children. A more detailed analysis is given in Table 4 which shows income tax and surtax as a percentage of gross income by points on the earnings distribution, and according to family size, for the period 1954/55 to 1974/75.

**FIGURE 1**
**INCOME TAX FOR THE SINGLE PERSON AS A PERCENTAGE OF TOTAL INCOME FOR THE LOW-PAID, AVERAGE AND HIGHER-PAID WORKER, 1954/5 to 1974/5**

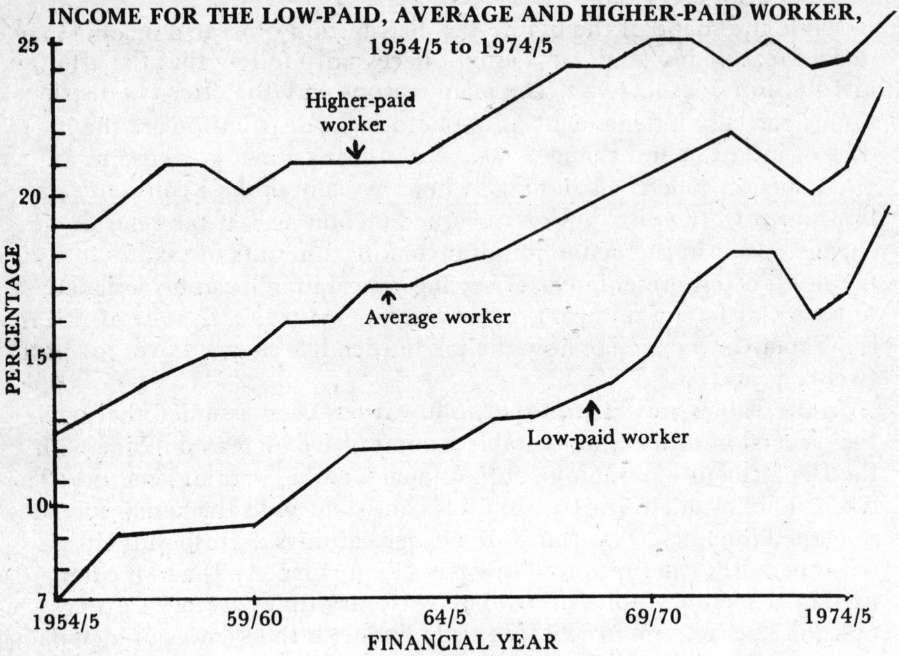


**FIGURE 2**
**INCOME TAX FOR FAMILIES WITH CHILDREN AS A PERCENTAGE OF TOTAL INCOME 1965/6 – 1974/5**

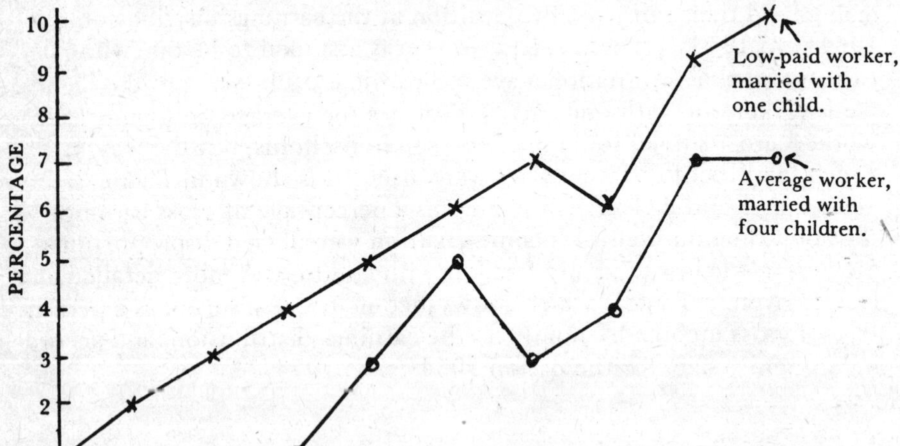

## *The Period 1954/55 to 1974/75*

Over the twenty years 1954/55 to 1974/75 there have been three distinct changes in the proportion of income taken in direct taxation.

First, there has been a general increase in the proportion of income paid as direct taxes at all points on the earnings distribution, and for all family sizes at each point.

Second, the lower end of the earnings distribution has experienced a larger percentage increase in the burden of taxation. A single man on two-thirds of average earnings pays three times more of his income in direct tax in 1974/75 than in 1954/55: an increase of 14 percentage points, from 7% of earnings to 21%. A single man whose earnings were twenty times the average only experienced an increase of 9 per cent, a rise of 6% points from 65% to 71% of gross income.

Third, at the bottom end of the earnings distribution the increase in the burden of taxation was larger the larger the family size. In 1954/55 a married couple with four children were only just subject to tax, if they earned income fifty per cent above average; by 1974/75 one fifth of earned income would have been paid in direct tax. Furthermore, while in 1954/55 a married couple with four children had just become subject to income tax at fifty per cent above average income, a family of the same size pays tax at two-thirds of average earnings in 1974/75.

Clearly, while there has been a general increase in the burden of taxation over the past twenty years the tax system has become less progressive. The low-paid, particularly those with children, have borne a disproportionate part of the increased general level of taxation. A comparison of the changes in the burden of taxation over the past twenty years based upon end points disguises short-run changes. Indeed there does appear to be a marked difference in the way different income levels fared under Labour and Conservative governments.

### *1954/55 to 1964/65*

Between the above two dates a Conservative government was in office and the tax system shifted in a less progressive direction. At two thirds of average income there was a five percentage point *increase* in the proportion of income paid in direct tax by a single man, while at twenty times average earnings there was a *reduction* of six percentage points. (At ten times average earnings the reduction was larger, ten percentage points.) Furthermore, at the bottom end of the earnings distribution families that hitherto had paid no direct tax were being drawn into the tax system.

## TABLE 4
## INCOME TAX AND SURTAX AS A PERCENTAGE OF INCOME: BY SIZE OF INCOME AND FAMILY EXPENDITURE

| | | *1954/5* | *1964/5* | *1970/71* | *1973/4* | *1974/75* |
|---|---|---|---|---|---|---|
| 2/3 of average earnings | s | 7 | 12 | 18 | 17 | 21 |
| | m | 2 | 6 | 12 | 14 | 16 |
| | 2c | 0 | 0 | 4 | 7 | 9 |
| | 4c | 0 | 0 | 0 | 4 | 4 |
| 80% | s | 9 | 15 | 21 | 20 | 23 |
| | m | 4 | 9 | 16 | 16 | 19 |
| | 2c | 0 | 1 | 9 | 11 | 13 |
| | 4c | 0 | 0 | 4 | 8 | 8 |
| 90% | s | 11 | 17 | 22 | 21 | 24 |
| | m | 6 | 11 | 18 | 18 | 21 |
| | 2c | 0 | 3 | 10 | 13 | 15 |
| | 4c | 0 | 0 | 6 | 11 | 11 |
| Average | s | 12 | 18 | 23 | 22 | 25 |
| | m | 7 | 13 | 19 | 19 | 22 |
| | 2c | 1 | 5 | 15 | 15 | 17 |
| | 4c | 0 | 0 | 9 | 12 | 13 |
| 130% | s | 16 | 21 | 25 | 24 | 27 |
| | m | 11 | 17 | 22 | 22 | 24 |
| | 2c | 4 | 10 | 18 | 18 | 21 |
| | 4c | 0 | 3 | 15 | 17 | 18 |
| 150% | s | 19 | 22 | 26 | 24 | 28 |
| | m | 13 | 19 | 23 | 23 | 26 |
| | 2c | 6 | 12 | 20 | 20 | 22 |
| | 4c | 1 | 6 | 17 | 18 | 20 |
| twice average | s | 23 | 24 | 28 | 26 | 29 |
| | m | 19 | 22 | 26 | 25 | 27 |
| | 2c | 12 | 16 | 23 | 22 | 25 |
| five times average | s | 35 | 28 | 37 | 38 | 44 |
| | m | 34 | 27 | 36 | 37 | 43 |
| | 2c | 31 | 25 | 34 | 35 | 41 |
| ten times average | s | 50 | 40 | 54 | 52 | 60 |
| | m | 49 | 39 | 53 | 52 | 59 |
| | 2c | 48 | 37 | 52 | 51 | 58 |
| twenty times average | s | 65 | 59 | 72 | 64 | 71 |
| | m | 65 | 59 | 72 | 63 | 71 |
| | 2c | 64 | 58 | 71 | 63 | 70 |

s = single persons
m = married couples
2c = married couples with two children ( under 11)
4c = married couples with four children (under 11)

The earned income of a married couple is assumed to be the husband's – where any of the income is earned by the wife the tax payable will be less than the amount shown.

For 1970/71, 1973/74 and 1974/75 the effect of 'clawback' on family allowances has been taken into account.

The income levels for each year are based on the average weekly earnings of men in the Department of Employment's October earnings enquiry. For October 1974 this is estimated as being £49 a week.

### *1964/65 – 1970/71*

The above two dates approximately correspond to a period of Labour Government, and there is a general increase in the burden of taxation at all points on the distribution. A single man on two thirds of average earnings experienced an increase of six percentage points in the proportion of his income paid in direct tax, at twenty times average earnings the increase was thirteen percentage points. While on this basis it appears that the tax system became more progressive it must be remembered that a six percentage point increase represents a fifty per cent increase in the amount of tax paid on two thirds of average earnings; at twenty times average earnings an increase of thirteen percentage points represents an increase of twenty-two per cent in the amount of tax paid. Clearly people with earnings at lower points on the distribution may feel that they were bearing the brunt of increased taxation. Furthermore, the tendency in the previous sub-period for low-paid families with children to enter the net of taxation at progressively lower rates of income continued unabated.

### *1970/71 to 1973/74*

This period approximately corresponds to a period of Conservative government; as in their earlier period of office the tax system became markedly less progressive. At the bottom end of the earnings distribution single persons experienced a slight decline in the burden of taxation: approximately one percentage point. However, single persons with earnings twenty times above average experienced a decline of eight percentage points. Moreover, while married couples at the top end of the distribution experienced a decline in the burden of taxation of similar proportions to that of single persons, at the lower end of the distribution the tax burden of married couples with children increased. Over this sub-period the general tendency was for the high-income groups to keep a larger proportion of income after tax, while at the lower points there was some discrimination in favour of single persons while families with children experienced an increase in the burden of taxation.

*1973/74 to 1974/75*

During this period the initial effects of the present Labour government's taxation policy came into operation. The general picture is that the overall burden of taxation increased but within this the system became more progressive. Single persons on twenty times average earnings saw their tax burden increase by seven percentage points, virtually restoring the 1970 situation. Single persons on two thirds of average earnings experienced an increase of four percentage points in the proportion of income taken in tax. However, there is a reduced tendency for married couples with families to be drawn ever deeper into the tax net. Below average earnings the tax burden of a married couple with four children remained virtually static.

Clearly, the two main political parties have adopted divergent attitudes as to the distribution of the direct tax burden: the Conservatives displaying a distinct tendency to lighten the tax burden at the upper end of the earnings distribution, with Labour tending to increase it or at least restore the previous position. However, both Labour and Conservative governments have substantially increased the amount of tax at the lower end of the earnings distribution, particularly the burden borne by married couples with children. The main reason for this has been commented upon by other writers, namely the reduction in the number of reduced rates of taxation and their eventual elimination.

Two reduced rates of income tax were introduced in 1945, a situation which lasted until 1952 when a third reduced rate was introduced. In 1963 there was a reduction to just two reduced rates, while in 1969 this was reduced to one, until finally in 1970 the reduced rates were eliminated altogether. The effect of this was to ensure that when "fiscal drag" brought hitherto exempt points on the distribution of income into the tax net it did so at a rate which rapidly built up their tax burden. The combined effect of fiscal drag and the abolition of reduced tax rates is vividly illustrated by a consideration of tax thresholds.

*Tax thresholds*

Tax thresholds – the level at which tax starts being due – have received much attention in the past. Indeed the newspapers following each budget often have tables showing the changes that have occurred. The usual method presenting the evidence is, however, in a format such as "everyone earning under £54 a week will be better off today (after the Healey Budget) than yesterday (before it)". Such statements clearly do not, however, tell us much because they fail to take account of changes in earnings and prices over time. This sub-section shows what changes in the income tax threshold 1961/62 to 1974/75 meant after taking account of these other factors as well.

Because the threshold varies as between households of different sizes and composition we have shown the position for three illustrative types: a single person, a married couple with one child aged 12, and a married couple with four children aged 7, 10, 12 and 14. The changes in the tax threshold in money terms are shown in the top part of Figure 3; they are shown in real terms (i.e. after taking account of inflation) in the middle part of the Table; and they are shown in relation to national average earnings (i.e. after taking account of earnings and prices) in the bottom part. It is the bottom part which should be of most concern in assessing the adequacy of past policy and the needs of the future, although usually it is the top or middle parts which are actually referred to.

From Figure 3 (the bottom part) it can be seen that most people who maintained their same relative position in the earnings distribution faced a lowering of the tax threshold over the period 1961/62 to 1974/75. This was most serious in the case of the married couple with four children since the threshold was some 30% lower at the end of the period compared to the beginning, but the couple with one child also experienced a worsening of the situation of some 20% and only single workers improved their lot in this respect. Moreover, when one considers that it is not just the level at which tax starts to be due, but the rate of tax on the taxable income as well that determines the overall tax burdens then the picture looks even worse. This is because whereas say in 1961/2, for example, the first £60 of taxable income was charged at a rate of only 8.75%, in 1974/75 the lowest rate of tax was 33%.

### *National Insurance Contributions*

So far we have concentrated solely on income tax and surtax, but there is of course a further direct tax applied to employment incomes in the form of national insurance contributions. These have tended to be quite *regressive* in their impact, for three reasons:

(i) there has always been a flat-rate component (though this has become less significant over the post-war period);

(ii) incomes become liable for graduated contributions at a lower threshold (currently £9 weekly) than is the case for income tax; and

(iii) the graduated contributions cease to be earnings-related at a cut-off point (currently £62 weekly).

**FIGURE 3**
**MOVEMENTS IN THE TAX THRESHOLD, 1961/2 – 1974/5**

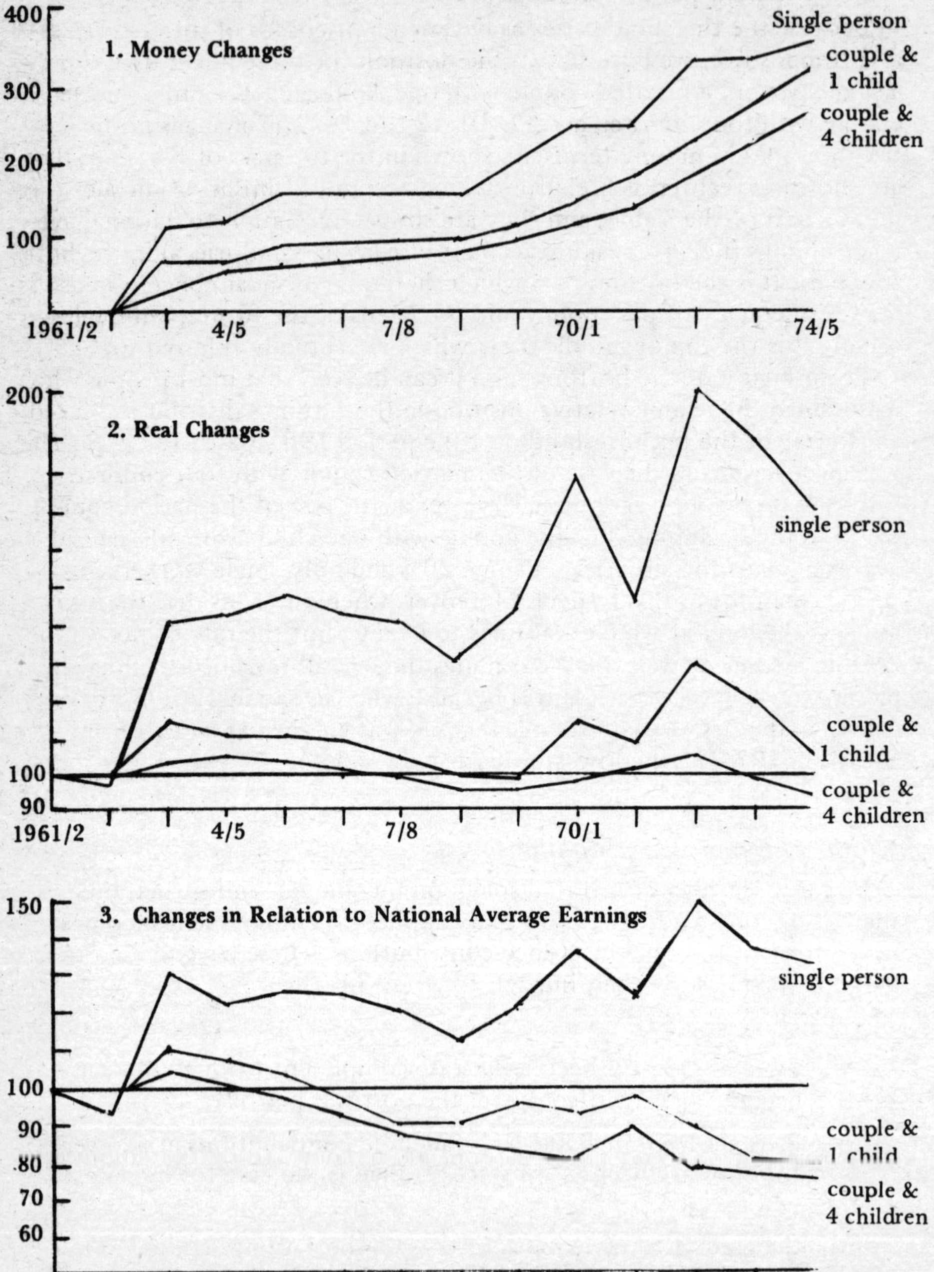

For these reasons the *combined* effects of income tax, surtax and national insurance contributions throw up a far less progressive incidence of direct taxation than was indicated in Table 4 above. The additional impact of national insurance contributions at 2/3 average earnings was 4.2% in 1954/55, 5.9% in 1964/65, and 6.2% in 1974/75; the impact at 130% of average earnings in the same years was 2.2%, 4.1% and 5.5%. (Full figures in relation to Table 4 can be provided on request.) The degree of regressiveness has thus been reduced over the period, and in April 1975 there will be a changeover to more fully earnings-related contributions, but social security contributions will nevertheless continue to moderate the more progressive structure of income tax liability. (Supporting evidence can be found in *Do Trade Unions Cause Inflation,* Jackson, Turner & Wilkinson, CUP 1972.)

*Summary and Implications*

Before drawing conclusions from the findings of this Section, attention has to be drawn to certain considerations:

1. Our figures are for cases where all income is earned by husbands. Increased employment of married women could either reduce or increase the share of the tax burden for families at the lower end of the distribution. This depends upon whether the growth in wives' employment has been proportionately greater at the lower end of the distributions, and whether the addition to the husbands' income has tended to equalise the overall distribution of incomes.

2. Inasmuch as earned income is not positively correlated with family size (and Family Expenditure Survey data suggest this can be the case), the disproportionate rate of increase of direct taxes on larger families will have a correspondingly inegalitarian impact upon the actual distribution of income after tax.

3. No overall attempt has been made to measure changes in *real* terms. There is evidence (from the Department of Employment's Pensioner Retail Price Indices and from studies on the lower-income family's price index by the Trade Union Research Unit and the Low Pay Research Unit) that inflation has – at least until recently – had a disproportionate impact upon lower-incomes. The distribution of *real* disposable incomes would thus show up as even less progressive than indicated in this Section. Moreover, since savings and investment income are associated with relatively higher incomes, it would be inappropriate to deflate the whole of the post-tax income of higher groups by a price index.

4. We have not dealt in any detail with investment income, which represents higher proportions of income at higher income levels. Tax changes over the period indicate however that a similar pattern would emerge. (We have however dealt with the concentration of wealth ownership in the previous Section and in our evidence on Income from Companies.)

5. Finally, it must of course be remembered that actual tax liability can be reduced by a whole range of allowances not fully investigated here (such as mortgage interest, life assurance and bank loan relief), which again are of considerably more significance at higher income levels. The extent to which a level of capital gains taxation lower than that for investment income can reduce actual liability should also be noted (an important example of this was covered in some detail by Section 4 of our Company Income Evidence).

There are several implications which emerge from this Section notwithstanding the above points. First, it is clear that governments *can* affect the formal structure of tax liability in more or less progressive directions. It can be shown that the current Government has a considerably further way to go if it is to reverse the reduced progressiveness of taxation on both earned and unearned income of the previous administration.

Second, the extent to which increased tax liability on lower incomes during the period covered now lies side by side with a complex and wide-ranging set of means-tested benefits represents not only a duplication of administrative effort but also a tendency towards a greater degree of regressiveness. This can be the result of high marginal rates of overall taxation as cut-off points and income-linked reductions combine with direct taxes, or of the low take-up of such benefits. We return to this area in Section 4.

Third, we doubt whether the progressiveness or otherwise of the tax system is entirely the result of deliberate decisions by Chancellors acting with accurate knowledge of the effects of their actions. The abolition of lower rates of taxation by Roy Jenkins in the latter sixties was intended to take a lot of people out of taxpaying brackets; the subsequent rate of inflation ensured however that such people then re-entered tax liability at the full marginal rate.

Following this, we would advocate consideration of the re-introduction of such lower rates of taxation for the first slices of taxable income. The principle could also be extended by reducing somewhat the very wide range of taxable income (currently up to £4,500) which is taxed at the standard rate (currently 33%) before surtax begins to apply. Both of these policies could significantly increase the degree of progressiveness in our tax structure; we have shown in this Section the degree to which this structure has tended to become less progressive over the period under consideration.

Attention should also be directed towards the possibility of more regularised adjustment of tax thresholds, in turn dependent upon the major allowances, in response to the rate of inflation.

It would be preferable for any such indexing process to have regard to movements in earnings and not just prices.

Our seventh recommendation is for the regressiveness of social security contributions to be examined, particularly in relation to the threshold and cut-off point.

Finally we would point out that there has been a shift in overall tax burdens away from the corporate sector and towards the personal sector in the post-war years. (Illustrated in Turner, Jackson and Wilkinson, *op. cit.*, and referred to also in our Evidence on Company Income.)

* * *

Mr. Healey, when introducing his November 1974 Budget, said that "The main instrument for achieving the necessary redistribution of wealth and income is our system of personal taxation. I do not intend to introduce legislation this autumn to deal with this issue: the time for dealing with this will be in the spring Budget". When he announces the new levels for the tax threshold, the size of the personal allowances, the rates of tax on different bends of taxable income, and his decision on whether and how to index the tax system, we hope he will have taken fully into account the overall changes in tax burdens during the last 20 years.

# 3

# Directors' Pay, other High Incomes, and Benefits

## Introduction

This section looks at the pay of directors and of other higher-paid company employees. (It is therefore relevant to the Royal Commission's "Higher Incomes" Reference too.) This of course excludes many professional people, barristers, doctors, accountants, who perhaps should be the subject of a separate study. A later paper will be looking at the justification of high incomes and that is the appropriate place in which to discuss the role of income as a component of ascribed social status in different occupations.

### *Three Company Case Studies*

We look first at three companies, one in textile manufacture and two in machine tools and study the way in which remuneration takes place.

The critical question in each case, is how the relative benefits to the company and to its controllers of distributed profits are likely to conflict with personal desires to maximise income. Tax policy will obviously play a large part in this and as a separate exercise the pros and cons of share option schemes are being examined. (TGWU Company Income Evidence.)

*Tootal* paid their 12 directors £158,104 (£13,200 each) but the chairman got £25,088, twice the average, and seven directors got more than £10,000 with three getting more than £15,000. In addition a further 10 employees received more than £10,000. The accounts do not say how much is set aside for "top hat" pensions but the total cost for past service pensions in 1973 was £4,077,000. In terms of equity interest the directors held between them 90,627 fully paid-up shares and another 226,400 in share options under a share purchase scheme. This represents a total wealth holding by the directors of £80,757 which would have gained them £5,660 in total. Again the chairman, Sir Neville Butterworth, was in a slightly better position, holding 83,621 shares yielding £1,469. Thus his total from the company was £26,557 of which his estimated net pay would be £13,000, again ten times the average pre-tax pay of his employees.

*Stone-Platt* list in their accounts the other directorships held by their directors. We thus know that the President is also a director of the Midland Bank. Sir Peter Aitken is on the board of Norwich Union Insurance and Skefco, H.R. Moore is chairman of Associated Engineering and Staveley Industries as well as a director of Hill Samuel, while R.W. Holder is managing director of the Fairey Company and on the board of the English Industrial Estates Company. It will no doubt be possible to assess their remuneration from these jobs in addition to their pay from Stone-Platt. The company does not list the total remuneration in terms of fees and salaries but the chairman got £13,485 and the highest paid director, presumably Sir Peter Aitken, £21,998. The distribution among the remainder was:-

**TABLE 1**

| *Salary Range* | *Number* |
|---|---|
| £20,000 – £22,500 | 1 |
| £17,500 – £20,000 | 1 |
| £15,000 – £17,500 | 2 |
| £2,500 – £5,000 | 2 |
| under £2,500 | 2 |

Between them the directors held £15,171 worth of shares yielding £1,204 or about £100 each which is not as much as in previous cases, contributing only a minor part towards Sir Peter Aitken's total gross pay of £22,200, which after tax was "only" six times the average pre-tax pay of all company employees.

*Mather & Platt* have only eight directors who shared £136,784 in 1973, including pension premiums, of which the chairman got £25,234 (excluding pension). Two directors also received between £25,000 and £27,500. Between them the eight hold 4.6% of the stock, a wealth of £289,240. Of this Sir William Mather holds £134, 435 and Douglas Paybody £104,968. The net gain in terms of share yield for the eight was £27,923, of which the Chairman received just under half and Mr. Paybody just over £10,000. Thus Sir William's total gross income was around £38,212, of which he would likely have taken home around £11,500: a mere 6½ times his workers' pre-tax pay.

*Directors' Remuneration*

The following data is taken from an INBUCON survey conducted in 1974:

**TABLE 2a**

**AVERAGE SALARY PAID TO MANAGING DIRECTORS IN 1972 AND 1973**

| *1972* | | | | *1973* | | | |
|---|---|---|---|---|---|---|---|
| *upper quartile* | *median* | *lower quartile* | *average* | *upper quartile* | *median* | *lower quartile* | *average* |
| 12,000 | 8,500 | 6,900 | 10,006 | 12,500 | 9,200 | 7,350 | 10,740 |
| | | | | *percentage change 1972-73* | | | |
| | | | | 4.2 | 8.2 | 6.5 | 7.4 |

**TABLE 2b**

**TOTAL REMUNERATION OF MANAGING DIRECTORS 1972 AND 1973**

| *upper quartile* | *median* | *lower quartile* | *average* | *upper quartile* | *median* | *lower quartile* | *average* |
|---|---|---|---|---|---|---|---|
| 12,500 | 9,000 | 7,116 | | 13,520 | 10,000 | 7,750 | |
| | | | | *percentage change* | | | |
| | | | | 8.5 | 11.0 | 10.3 | |

It is clear that increases in "pay" have largely come through in the form of "extras" rather than salary; as is confirmed by the falling proportion of total pay represented by salary:

**TABLE 2c**

**SALARY AS A % AGE OF TOTAL REMUNERATION**

| *1972* | | | *1973* | | |
|---|---|---|---|---|---|
| *upper quartile* | *median* | *lower quartile* | *upper quartile* | *median* | *lower quartile* |
| 96 | 94.5 | 97 | 92.5 | 92 | 93.5 |

We noted above that the total remuneration exceeded "salary" by about 10%, some of which excess would be free of tax.

We have to make some sort of distinction between the executive and the non-executive director. Whereas the former has a day-to-day function within the company (head of division or whatever), the latter usually acts in a consultancy or advisory capacity. There has been a tendency in fact in recent years to use non-executive directors to an increasing extent in a functional role and their number has increased accordingly. A BIM survey* noted that in the five years 1967-1971 the number of non-executive appointments had exceeded retirements by 40% and that the majority of companies in their survey had made such appointments.

**TABLE 3**

**BACKGROUND OF NON-EXECUTIVE DIRECTORS APPOINTED 1967-1971 WITH % AGE OF COMPANIES INVOLVED**

| | | | |
|---|---|---|---|
| retired executive director of company | 41% | accountancy | 22½% |
| family or historic connection with company | 33% | lawyers | 31½% |
| banking and finance | 56% | politicians | 13% |
| technical specialities | 18½% | substantial shareholding | 17½% |

(50% of these were titled and *none* were women).

We suspect that the ex-director and those with other connections are unlikely to be active in seeking more progressive policies; probably quite the opposite. As this practice is followed in three-quarters of the companies surveyed, a figure which includes 60 of the top companies in the UK, one must seriously question its role. For instance, while of minimal concern in this particular exercise, what are to be the likely reactions of boards so constituted to increasing industrial democracy or worker monitoring of managerial efficiency?

On the other hand few would question the value, from a company point of view, of having persons with financial or legal experience though it is a matter of some regret that during the period covered by the survey this experience did not manifest itself in the form of a more dynamic industrial attitude, as home investment levels sank ever lower. In a period of technological advance it is worth noting that less than 20% of companies felt it necessary to appoint those with such skills and one must hopefully assume that the executive directors would have redressed the balance in this direction. The fact that 17½% of directors buy their way into the boardroom is a trifle disquieting, as is the number of politicians. In terms of company strategy both of these no doubt make good sense, though one wonders what it was in Duncan Sandys' hapless political career that made him so attractive to the board of Lonhro – his "knowledge" of Africa perhaps?

In total 75% were ex-public school (Eton & Winchester being the most popular) and 60% were products of Oxbridge. Again we have to ask how this will assist the process of assimilation of worker directors given the somewhat different social backgrounds and the lack of awareness of daily problems faced by the majority of such people.

---

* *The Board of Directors*, Management Survey Report no. 10, BIM 1972.

*Multi-Directorships*

The BIM survey found that the average pay of non-executive directors was £1,614 in 1971, though no enquiries were made in terms of equity holding. What the survey did show was that over 15% held more than ten *other* directorships and that half of these had more than 20. Given that it is normally company policy to discourage its executive directors from being involved elsewhere, it is a safe assumption that the majority of these were in other non-executive posts. For anyone holding 20 directorships, at the average rate of remuneration in 1971, their income would have been £32,280 including fees. Among these, of course, would be some getting very much more but we only have reliable figures for the aggregates. This is an area where further investigation by the Royal Commission would be necessarily welcome; company law reform proposals have devoted a lot of attention to the need to regulate nominee shareholdings and inside dealings.

Returning to one of our case studies (Stone-Platt), we find that of the four lowest-paid directors (presumably the non-executive ones), two got less than £2,500 and two got between £2,500 and £5,000 in 1973. In addition they held between them 35,834 shares worth £7,000 face value, from which they netted £900. Thus in this particular case the average gain from the company was around £1,750 each.

Multi-directorships in fact have a very important effect not only on the accumulation of income but equally on the way the incomes of employees earning far less are derived. For example the motor giant British Leyland plays a vital role in the economy and has under its influence the livelihoods of thousands of workers, their families, communities indeed and regions. Yet one wonders how the directors of British Leyland can properly deploy their own resources when between them they have 83 directorships. Lord Stokes has twenty two, including the National Westminster Bank, in addition to his post of Chairman of British Leyland which earned him £47,915. J.N.R. Barker, who is probably the highest paid director, has slightly less direct salary and ten other directorships. He was also granted an option in 1967 to buy for £40,281 a company house in which he was living at the time under a leasing arrangement. Finally in March of last year he exercised this option. Sir David Barran has thirteen directorships including Shell, BICC, Burton Group, Glaxo, General Accident, Midland Bank plus various finance companies. Among the other directors is the ubiquitous J.D. Slater whose advice to all investors last year was to "get out of stocks and go into money."*

---

* For example: 15/11/74 he reaffirmed his belief in cash by selling his Hong Kong subsidiary (*Financial Times* 16/11/74).

It is possible that the diverse interests of the policy makers on the board have played an important part in its present troubles. Considering that many of these directorships are in overseas associates and subsidiaries, the reason for the very poor performance of BL overseas may also lie in this quarter.

For instance how much of what has been estimated as £75 million invested in Australia and Spain will ever be recovered? When Authi, the Spanish subsidiary, is eventually sold, either to General Motors or a government controlled consortium, the losses sustained will presumably eventually be underwritten by the long-term support announced by the Secretary of State for Industry on December 6th.

The point of all this is that it is impossible to separate the moral justifications for high incomes from the apparent inability of people with multiple directorships, which guarantee them even higher incomes, to safeguard the investments of which they are but temporary custodians.

One could cite Courtaulds as a further case in point. Here is a company employing one quarter of the workers in its industry, laying men off in one plant after another. Yet when one examines the 83 directorships that their board holds we find representation from Hill Samuel, GKN, EMI, Guinness Mahon, British Nuclear Fuels (in turn owned by the UKAEA, of which Lord Kearton is a member) and various British and foreign banking interests.

The lesson would appear to be identical. In other evidence on company income it was demonstrated how inextricably bound up are the fortunes of the whole with those of the parts.* However much one may wish to believe that personal engrandisement does not feature in the decision-making process, some of the involvements of directors suggest otherwise. Moreover, the degree of concentration of power, control and influence into few hands is extremely alarming, and certainly against the spirit of current intended reforms.

*Fringe Benefits*

One very important area to which often only tacit acknowledgement is conventionally given is what can broadly be termed "fringe benefits".

Companies will frequently use these in order to attract and retain employees, particularly senior management levels up to and including chairmen. Quite often they also apply to directors, not so much for this purpose as to supplement *post-tax* income and to add status. Their overriding advantage to the person receiving them is that while they are not

* TGWU Evidence on Company Income, Section 4.

immediately realisable in cash terms they do represent a net gain in income terms. This is because their availability reduces the burden on post-tax income that would otherwise have to be borne. Thus the real disposable income is increased, with a wider choice of preferences than would be available if the benefit were not provided but some cash settlement made in lieu. Thus they are doubly advantageous to the recipient.

It is thus necessary to examine what is the trend in this area and also to try and place a figure in general terms on the value of the benefit and the degree to which it supplements the "salary".

The benefits include "top hat" pensions, benefits paid to surviving dependants of employees, child allowances and death benefits, health and welfare services, severance pay and compensation for loss of property rights (the "golden handshake"), travel expenses, entertainment and clothing allowances, subsidised meals, cars, assistance with house purchase, hotel and holiday expenses, school fees, medical benefits and expenses. No doubt others come to light in particular circumstances; we have already referred (in Section 4 of our Company Income Evidence) to share option schemes.

By and large these benefits will accrue to the full-time directors and other senior personnel and most companies choose, according to another BIM survey,* those benefits that best fit in with company policy and outlook. Of course different people at different levels are offered different "packages" but the following table, taken from the survey, shows the eligibility within all the companies covered for different benefits:

**TABLE 4**

| *type of benefit* | *% age of managers eligible* |
|---|---|
| sick pay schemes | 99.9 |
| life assurance | 93.6 |
| contributory pension | 78.1 |
| accident insurance | 77.6 |
| dependants cover | 48.6 |
| disability benefit | 38.4 |
| BUPA etc. | 37.8 |
| non-contributory pension | 18.8 |
| overtime payments | 11.8 |
| "top hat" pensions | 4.6 |
| prizes | 3.9 |
| cash other than individual bonus | 3.0 |
| share option schemes | 1.3 |

* *Employee Benefits Today*, MSC no. 19, BIM 1974.

This quite clearly shows that companies are eager to protect the manager as a form of investment while "rewards" are given on a more limited basis. Nonetheless the much lower percentages refer to that section of senior management and directorate that immediately concern this brief i.e. persons on high incomes. However these BIM figures are at some variance with the results of a similar piece of research by INBUCON; the following data is their interpretation of the 1973 position:

**TABLE 5**

| *type of benefit* | *% age of managers covered* |
|---|---|
| subsidized lunches | 65.0 |
| sole use of company car | 55.2 |
| bonus | 30.1 |
| "top hat" pensions | 26.6 |
| BUPA | 26.4 |
| allowance for use of own car | 14.5 |
| assistance with house purchase | 6.3 |
| share purchase scheme | 5.1 |
| share option scheme | 2.5 |
| subsidised housing | 1.4 |

We would draw particular attention to the discrepancy between the respective figures for "top hat" pensions and for the BUPA scheme. This is in all probability due to a different method of surveying (eligibility as opposed to take-up). In the case of share option, although statistically one figure is twice the other, both surveys are identifying a relatively small group of people (perhaps no more than a dozen in each company, and not all companies adopt this policy anyway). These arithmetical differences do not prevent us from examining the potential value of the benefits, nor from drawing some general conclusions in such areas in which there is consistency in the data. The point can be made again that, given the salary ranges we are looking at, we are considering personnel whose entitlement to all types of benefit is greater than that of those below them in the hierarchy and the advantage that they accrue in this must also be noted.

The following short table illustrates the disparity in benefit availability for employees of a medium sized company and serves to underline not only the extra cash and money advantage but also the less determinate discrimination which inevitably accompanies such a policy.

**TABLE 6**

**TYPICAL BENEFIT AVAILABILITY TO EMPLOYEES OF ONE MEDIUM SIZED UK COMPANY**

| *benefit* | *top & middle management* | *supervisory & clerical* | *manual grades* |
|---|---|---|---|
| pension | contributory | contributory | state pension only |
| life assurance | annual salary x 3 | annual salary x 3 | none |
| sick pay | full pay for 10 weeks & half pay for a further 10 weeks | full pay for 8 weeks & half pay for a further 8 | £4/week for max.of 8 weeks after 2 years service |
| medical insurance | group scheme discount | | none |
| annual holiday | four weeks | | 3 weeks |
| house purchase assistance | bridging loans | | none |
| bonus | 10% of annual salary | none | production only |
| company car | top: £2,000 plus mid: £1,500 if needed by job | £1,000 if job requires | none |
| professional fees | paid in full | | none |
| subsidised meals | dining room | staff canteen | works canteen |
| early retirement option | available to all | | not available |

We have noted from previous figures that 'top' management (column one) are already receiving between 6 and 10 times the real pay of the manual workers; this relativity is considerably enhanced by the additional range of subsidies offered. A simple quantification could be made from this table alone but it would err on the side of conservatism. Nevertheless we can say that taking two individuals, one from the factory floor and another from the board room, both desiring to buy a house and both having a short period of sickness during the period, the former would be disadvantaged in absolute terms of the sum of around £600 or 25% of average earnings whilst already taking home around one-eighth of the pay of his board-room colleague.

We now go on to look at each benefit separately and to make some estimates of their true value in income equivalent terms.

### *The Car*

There are two ways in which a car may be provided. Either the director has the sole use of a company vehicle, sometimes with a chauffeur, or he may get an allowance for using his own car.

Much of his travel will be on company expense fuel, with wear and tear and other expenses normally covered. A man in this position is virtually guaranteed free motoring, which it can be argued is worth £12 – £15* per week, or even more.

Of course, where the car is provided, a substantial capital outlay (£2000 – £3000) is avoided – all of it free of tax.

*The House*

Assistance with house purchase or subsidised personal housing can take a variety of forms. At one extreme is the "tied cottage" of the agricultural worker; at the other, we have evidence from recent enquiries into the affairs of at least one company of quite substantial mansions being acquired for senior directors and chairmen (Lonhro, Pergamon Press). While there may be extremes, it does show how such facilities can be "extended" by those with the power to do so. Other companies provide bridging loans at low interest rates.**

One survey showed that 4½% of managing directors obtained assistance with house purchase and that just over 4% had subsidised housing of one sort or another. One can perhaps be forgiven for making the inevitable comparison with tied cottages for agricultural workers.

Under such arrangements, the reduction in the level of repayments that would otherwise be due to a building society, given current interest rates, can be in the order of £800 p.a. which can be seen as a direct post-tax income equivalent. In addition the recipient would still be entitled to claim tax relief on the loan from the company!

*The Holiday*

Companies are – to say the least – circumspect concerning their policy on holidays for their executives. It is not so much the duration, (though sometimes comparisons there are interesting), as the method of financing that concerns us. The Royal Commission may well wish to enquire to what extent senior management and their families have fully paid holidays under the guise of a legitimate business excursion. The General Secretary Designate of the Inland Revenue Staff Federation has recently indicated that this practice is far more widespread than hitherto had been considered.

In terms of the actual length of holiday the right of all working people to sufficient rest and leisure is something that we would not

---

* A.A. estimate.

** A good example, with staff employees offered loans as low as 3% together with removal expenses, can be found in the INBUCON survey, *op. cit.*

question. However, further iniquities emerge on comparing the practice for executives with that for manual workers.

Unlike most other places in Europe, Britain has no legal provision as to the minimum amount of paid holiday. It has been left to custom and practice to establish the present situation whereby 94% of manual men and 90% of manual women have entitlements of at least three weeks. Of these, 75% are under 4 weeks, so the majority of people are getting between 15-18 days paid holiday per year. Some companies insist that the three weeks are not taken together because of production problems, whilst others frown on odd days being taken.

In this context it is interesting to note that INBUCON found that in 1973 three-quarters of all executives had paid leave from 20-24 days, and that 20% had over five weeks. Of those having more than 30 or more days (six weeks), 50% were in the range with a basic salary of £10,000 or more. The BIM survey noted that 5% of the largest companies offered 26 days or more to their senior management and that a further 10% used "private arrangements".

It is difficult to give an income equivalent for a holiday save to say that for the recipient a longer paid holiday is clearly beneficial and that it can reduce the time lost to the company and the individual due to work-based stress.

*Lunches, Hotels, Travel etc.*

Most companies pay all reasonable expenses incurred in the course of business without question for their senior staff. The following example is of a company in the distributive trade with under 1000 employees in 1973. It gives the cost payments authorised for directors and senior management.

**TABLE 7**
**ACCOMMODATION, MEALS AND ALLOWANCES**

| | *London & Europe* | *U.K. Eire* | *Rail Fare* | *Air Fare* | *Float allowance* |
|---|---|---|---|---|---|
| Hotel | £12.00 | £9.75 | 1st c. | Tourist | £50 |
| Dinner | £5.75 | £4.50 | | | |
| Lunch | £3.25 | £2.25 | | | |
| Breakfast | £2.25 | £1.75 | | | |
| Overnight stay with friends | £6.00 | £4.90 | | | |
| Daily allowance outside Europe | £12.50 | | | | |

These reimbursements by and large represent out-of-pocket expenses, but there are obvious opportunities for small gains here and there (how many people charge £6.00 a night to their friends?). Assuming a reasonable amount of travel, say once a week, the amount saved plus the net gain from the reduced cost of normal social intercourse could be around £200 p.a.

*Other items*

Among the other quantifiable benefits are such things as telephone allowances, possibly worth £70 p.a. free medical insurance (£50) entertainment and dress allowances (£100) and school fees (£380 on average).

Many fringe benefits are not directly realisable in terms of transfer of responsibility for capital outlay. The "medicare" facilities for instance apply mainly when one is sick. BUPA is of course kept alive by company payments but perhaps this is not the right forum to discuss the merits or otherwise of a private health service. Private health schemes are popular with companies because they avoid the delays in the NHS (in part caused by under investment because of the existence of a private health sector*).

*Pensions*

These can be contributory or non-contributory; the "top hat" pension additionally includes severance pay. This is a device for compensating for loss of earnings potential and again invites a comparison with ordinary workers, this time through the provisions of the Redundancy Payments Act.**

The pension is normally linked to final salary and just under half of all managing directors in the BIM survey were entitled to "top hat" pensions. This gives considerably enhanced payment benefits, sometimes protected against inflation. We can value this (against what it would cost in terms of ordinary saving out of salary) at around £200 p.a.

*Share Option* and share purchase schemes allow senior management to acquire equity at a lower rate than that operating on the market. During periods of high share prices this has a considerable capital value but principally the benefit derives from distributed profits. Scrip issues have been dealt with in Section 4 of our Company Income Evidence.

---

* Survey results demonstrating the very wide application of company health arrangements are to be found in the BIM survey on Executive Health Care.

** We have drawn attention to wide discrepancies in this general area in section 2 of our evidence on Company Income.

*Bonus systems*

Bonuses as a form of service can be based on profit, turnover or performance.

One third of managing directors receive bonuses as a percentage of their actual salary and in 1973 this was worth on average £2,981; 64.2% of these were based on profit, 32.5% on performance, 2.5% on turnover and 0.8% on profit plus performance.* (Bonuses are of course taxable.)

*Cost of benefits*

The results of a BIM enquiry into the cost of fringe benefits showed that as a percentage of the annual payroll bill most companies calculated this to be less than 20% (see below). However, one medium sized company with a "sophisticated" benefits policy reckoned that the average cost for manual employees was 20% of the payroll while for top management it was 40%.**

In the USA the overall average is around 30% and in some countries in Europe, where social security is a company responsibility, it is nearer 50%.***

**TABLE 8**
**COMPANY ESTIMATES OF COST OF EMPLOYEE BENEFITS**
**(from BIM survey)**

| | *cost as percentage of annual payroll* | | | | |
|---|---|---|---|---|---|
| | 0-10% | 10-15% | 15-20% | 20-30% | over 30% |
| % of companies | 47 | 21 | 16 | 12 | 4 |

*Summary of Fringe Benefits*

The following is the list of fringe benefits in Section Three of our Evidence, with estimated values and sources of information.

**TABLE 9**

| ITEM | SOURCE OF INFORMATION | ESTIMATED VALUE OF BENEFIT £ |
|---|---|---|
| The Car | Automobile Association & BIM Survey (incl. capital repayments over 2 years) | 2,200 |
| House | INBUCON Survey & Halifax Building Society | 800 |

* Employee Benefits Today, BIM, *op. cit.*
** BIM Survey, *op. cit.*
*** E.E.C. and U.S. Bureau of Statistics.

| *Item* | *Source of information* | *Estimated value of benefit* £ |
|---|---|---|
| Expenses | Various Surveys BIM & INBUCON | 200 |
| Telephone | Post Office | 70 |
| Health Insurance | BUPA | 50 |
| Entertainment & dress | Various Surveys | 100 |
| School fees | DES Approved List of Residential Schools | 380 |
| Pension | BIM Survey | 200 |
| Holiday | Valued estimate | 400 |
| | TOTAL | £4,300 |

### *Total benefit to executives*

Gathering together all the valuations made above of fringe benefits and assuming, safely at least for 4% of directors, that they are in receipt of them all, we find that the monetary value is around £4,300 p.a. tax free. At higher marginal rates of taxation the pre-tax equivalent income becomes very substantial indeed. This is well in excess of the normal pre-tax income of most of the workers in the companies involved. Doubtless the Royal Commission will express its own view on this but in the name of equity a substantial reform of the law governing these matters would appear to be vital. The redistributive effect towards higher income is an immediate cause for concern but their existence does also raise profound questions of social justice. We have already touched upon the health service but we could have noted that at a time when energy conservation is deemed paramount, the large capacity motor cars used by companies may be a luxury we cannot afford.

We cannot but applaud the augmentation of statutory provisions for sickness, bereavement and retirement but this union in common with many others has experienced great difficulty in convincing companies that this policy should be extended to all their employees. Again we note the differentiation that is made and its adversely distributive effect. One possible first step would be to make all such benefits taxable and for companies not to be able to set the cost of them against tax. This would go some way to reducing the obvious iniquities that exist at present.

# 4

# Some Wider Considerations

So far attention has been directed towards the overall patterns of income and wealth distribution, and the incidence of taxation upon them. There are however sources of data other than the Inland Revenue, and issues other than those so far identified, which can be of relevance to the Royal Commission. These are dealt with – mostly briefly – in this Section.

*Earnings Data*

Our main source of information on the distribution of earnings is the Department of Employment's New Earnings Survey. Whilst representing a considerable improvement upon what was previously available, this Survey nevertheless has serious limitations:

(i) Coverage has been reduced since the first Survey in 1968; although age and make-up of pay analyses have now been reinstated, there are several areas (such as occupational pensions) which are omitted but which could be of immense help in assessing income distribution.

(ii) The timing and backdating of settlements is not identified in the Survey, but are crucial to any assessment of changes over time. and between groups.

(iii) The Survey offers a "snapshot" picture of a particular pay week. It has been indicated (Cyril Leach* of NEDO's paper to Statistics Users Conference, 1973) that this overstates implied annual earnings; the question of lifecycle earnings (to which we return in Section 5) is also relevant here.

(iv) There is no published data referring to company level, which is crucial from a private sector collective bargaining viewpoint. The

* *A General view of Data on Wages*, Labour Statistics, NEDO, 1973.

Department of Employment has agreed to provide this data when requested by both employer and union(s), but the former's co-operation is not commonly forthcoming. (This area is relevant to our discussion of disclosure of information in Section 5 of our Company Income Evidence).

(v) Finally, and perhaps most important, is that there is no way in which NES data can be matched with either Inland Revenue Statistics or Family Expenditure data. The unit is the individual employee, not the tax unit or the family. Any progress which could be made in linking these sources would be invaluable to researchers. (Again we return to this problem in Section 5.)

*Wage Rate Data*

We are much worse off in terms of useful information about wage rates than earnings. The official Department of Employment Indices are questionably constructed; they refer to minimum entitlements as well as minimum rates; and they give rise to confusions of interpretation (see Moore, Hughes and Gregory* in *Labour Statistics, op.cit.*). We have no adequate data on conventional or standard weekly pay, which amongst other reasons makes international comparisons quite impossible (see *Earnings, Wages and Labour Costs: Some Problems of International Comparisons,* Trade Union Research Unit 1974). The questions of consistency, comparability and harmonisation with regard to pay data between different countries are crucial to any serious analysis of relative distributions between different countries.
NB: The question of *Equal Pay,* which is very much part of this area of earnings and wage rates, is dealt with in detail in an Appendix to this Evidence.

*Family Expenditure Survey*

Apart from the question of the adequacy of sample size, the main consideration arising here is the possibility of linking with other sources of data (to which we return in Section 5). We have serious doubts about the way in which FES data is used both in the construction of the Retail Price Index (reservations were mentioned in Section 2), and in the analysis constituting the annual articles on *"Incidence of Taxation and Benefits"* in *Economic Trends.* This latter is given our more detailed consideration below.

---

* A critical view of the utility of government statistics on collective bargaining.

*Real Disposable Income*

The only official data in this area are CSO aggregates; no attempt is made to undertake analyses for different income levels or different family composition. The incidence of direct taxation, the rate of inflation and – at the lower end of the income distribution – entitlement to means-tested benefits (which we understand exceed 40 in number) represent a powerful combination of forces determining the effective distribution of real disposable income. It appears to us to be a paramount requirement for official indices to be constructed, not only in the interests of adequate analysis of real income distribution, but also from the point of view of the "social wage" and indeed the "social contract". The official response to proposals from the Trade Union Research Unit and others for such indices (see *Labour Statistics,* NEDO, *op. cit.*) appeared favourable, but there appears to have been no progress in this direction. Our suspicion is that such data would provide evidence of inequalities in the distribution of income in excess of those indicated by conventional Inland Revenue data – and the latter are pronounced enough.*

*Incidence of Taxation and Benefits*

In previous sections the distribution of income both before and after tax was examined. However, it can be argued that this is only a partial picture of the myriad of factors which affect people's living standards. Many of the government's social welfare policies such as education and the national health service, together with indirect taxation, also affect the distribution of income.

A comparatively recent source of information about overall trends in income distribution is that developed by J.L. Nicholson and continued by the Central Statistical Office (CSO). The CSO data is published annually in *Economic Trends* and provides a reasonably coherent picture of changes in taxation and benefits at least since 1961. The information collected in the course of the Family Expenditure Survey provides the basis upon which direct and indirect taxes, and direct and indirect benefits are allocated to different income levels and types of household. Since the basis is a sample survey, allowance has to be made for year to year fluctuations attributable to sampling error. Moreover, there are fundamental defects in the way in which the CSO analysis is compiled and presented. However, before elaborating upon the latter, it is interesting to examine the trends revealed by the CSO data.

---

* See for instance "Low Pay and Fiscal Pay", R. Moore, in *Low Pay,* ed. Frank Field, Arrow 1973.

a) *Average incomes 1961-73*

Table 1 shows what has been happening to the average incomes before and after tax of various types of household.

**TABLE 1**

**AVERAGE INCOMES BEFORE AND AFTER TAXES & BENEFITS**

| | **Income after all taxes and benefits as a percentage of original income** | | | **growth 1961-1973 (1961 = 100)** | |
|---|---|---|---|---|---|
| | *1961* | *1969* | *1973* | *original income* | *income after taxes & benefits* |
| 1 adult | (109) | 107 | 119 | 250 | 272 |
| 1 adult non-retired | (89) | 84 | 93 | 251 | 265 |
| 2 adults, 1 child | (82) | 77 | 80 | 263 | 257 |
| 2 adults, 2 children | (91) | 84 | 86 | 269 | 252 |
| 2 adults, 3 children | (104) | 95 | 96 | 299 | 275 |
| 2 adults, 4 children | (109) | 107 | 112 | 257 | 264 |

*Note:* figures in brackets are estimated.

Source: *Economic Trends* December 1974, Table 5, plxx

The main points of interest are:-

(i) There is a general pattern of a slight reduction in income after all taxes and benefits as a percentage of original income throughout the 1960's. Since then there has been a slight improvement, in some cases more than restoring the 1961 relativity.

(ii) There is a tendency for the relative position after taxes and benefits of households composed of a married couple plus one, two or three children to deteriorate in relation to other types of household.

(iii) The growth rates of original incomes and incomes after tax and benefits clearly indicate that the system of taxes and benefits has been leaning most heavily upon married couples with one to three children. On the other hand there has been a considerable boost to the income of all single adults and, to a lesser extent, single adults (non-retired) and married couples with four children.

The general conclusion from the data in Table 1 is that between 1961 and 1973 there is an overall tendency for the system of taxation and benefits to favour pensioners while being less generous to households with between one and three children.

b) *Medians and quintiles*

An examination of averages can illustrate changes in the impact of taxation as between different types of household, but does not illustrate changes *within* these types. Information on the median and upper and lower quintiles is shown in Table 2.

**TABLE 2**

**INCOME AFTER TAXES AND BENEFITS AS A PERCENTAGE OF ORIGINAL INCOME; MEDIAN, FIRST QUINTILE AND FOURTH QUINTILE**

| | *1st quintile* | *median* | *4th quintile* |
|---|---|---|---|
| 1 adult | | | |
| 1961 | 186 | 84 | 80 |
| 1968 | 351 | 184 | 71 |
| 1969 | 387 | 203 | 75 |
| 1973 | 502 | 234 | 80 |
| 2 adults, 2 children | | | |
| 1961 | 92 | 92 | 88 |
| 1968 | 87 | 85 | 85 |
| 1969 | 89 | 86 | 78 |
| 1973 | 89 | 88 | 84 |
| 2 adults, 4 children | | | |
| 1961 | 121 | 112 | 110 |
| 1968 | 122 | 110 | 106 |
| 1969 | 128 | 115 | 98 |
| 1973 | 125 | 120 | 101 |
| 1 adult (excluding pensioners)* | | | |
| 1969 | 130 | 78 | 69 |
| 1973 | 128 | 78 | 74 |

*Note:* there was a change in the definition of original income from 1969 onwards.

---

* The category '1 adult' (excluding pensioners) was not included in the analysis in the years prior to 1967

The main features of Table 2 are:-

(i) that with the exception of one-adult households the impact of taxes and benefits has not been markedly different throughout the individual distributions. Thus, while for other types of households the net effects of taxation and benefits have been broadly similar over the period 1961-73, one-adult households have exhibited a marked improvement in the relative position of the lowest quintile while the highest quintile remained static.
(ii) The relative improvement in the position after taxes and benefits of one-adult households revealed in Table 1 is entirely due to an improvement at the bottom end of the distribution.
(iii) The net impact of taxes and benefits is progressive: i.e., income after all taxes and benefits is a higher percentage of original income after all taxes and benefits at the lowest quintile than it is at the highest decile. (However, *all* taxes as a percentage of original income plus cash benefits are not particularly progressive; in some income bands married couples with children pay a greater proportion in taxes than single adults (Table 4 (iii) *Economic Trends*).)

It has already been mentioned that there are defects in the CSO analysis, particularly the treatment of the distribution of benefits between income bands. Unfortunately the published data upon which Tables 1 and 2 are based does not allow a more detailed examination of the factors which determine income after taxes and benefits. However, the way in which the income levels are determined does lend itself to a similar treatment to that used in Section 2 illustrating the impact of income tax and surtax on a stable distribution of income.

c) *Constant relationship with average earnings*

The intervals between income bands in the CSO analysis are approximately twenty-one per cent; thus every time average earnings rise by twenty-one per cent, or some compound of this, a household will, if it maintains a constant relationship with average earnings, move up one or more income bands. There are two periods over which the rise in average earnings (based on the October enquiry) closely approximates to a move between CSO income bands:-

1962 to 1970, when average earnings rose by 77 per cent,
a movement through three income bands;
1970-1973, when average earnings rose by 46 per cent,
a movement through two income bands.

Unfortunately the 1962 and 1970 analyses are not comparable. Changes in the definition of original income and the way in which benefits are distributed between income bands render all but a few limited comparisons invalid. However, one category that has remained reasonably intact between the two dates is income tax and surtax. Changes in the amount of income tax and surtax paid within comparable income bands is shown in Table 3.

Table 3 shows that the burden of income taxation has grown at a much faster rate than the rise in incomes. While income rose by 77 per cent income tax and surtax paid rose by over 200 per cent; in percentage terms the increase was greater for married couples with children than for single persons.

Between 1970 and 1973 there has been little change in any of the main components of the CSO analysis; thus a more detailed analysis can be undertaken. Table 4 shows income after taxes and benefits as a percentage of original income in 1970 and 1973 for comparable income bands. Overall there has been a slight increase in income after taxes and benefits as a percentage of original income. However, there are deviations from this pattern, particularly at lower income levels where the pattern is reversed.

It can be shown that the burden of income tax is rising faster than incomes in the lower income bands. A married couple with two children within the income band £988-£1196 paid £39 in income tax in 1970. A similar household in the equivalent income band (£1446-£1749) paid £78 in income tax. The latter represents a doubling of the amount of tax paid for a household maintaining a constant relationship with average earnings. The pattern of greater proportionate increases in the burden of taxation for the lower income bands is also evident for other households with children. This result confirms the findings in Section 2 of our evidence which showed that income tax liability was increasing for low-paid workers with children.

d) *Pensions*

A detailed examination of the data published *Economic Trends* also shows that for married couples with children the inclusion of a pensioner household in any one year can cause large fluctuations in the effect of taxes and benefits. For married couples with two children in the income band £816-£988 pensions added £72 to original income during 1970, while in the equivalent income band in 1973 they contributed nothing. The inclusion of a category as volatile as pensions can and does lead to misleading results and is best left out of the main analysis.

## TABLE 3

### INCOME TAX AND SURTAX PAID AT "EQUIVALENT" INCOMES, 1962 AND 1970

£ annual

| Ranges of Gross Income | | 260- | 315- | 382- | 460- | 559- | 676- | 816- | 988- | 1196- | 1448- |
|---|---|---|---|---|---|---|---|---|---|---|---|
| | 1970 | 460- | 559- | 676- | 816- | 988- | 1196- | 1448- | 1752- | 2122- | 2566- |
| 1 adult | 1962 | 24.1 | 44.3 | 29.1 | 51.0 | 51.1 | 71.1 | 110.4 | | | |
| | 1970 | 55 | 81 | 98 | 161 | 171 | 252 | 294 | | | |
| 2 adults + 2 children | 1962 | - | - | - | - | 2.0 | 16.1 | 23.3 | 67.4 | 85.7 | 140.2 |
| | 1970 | | | | 14 | 39 | 113 | 170 | 229 | 290 | 448 |
| 2 adults + 3 children | 1962 | - | - | - | - | 8.5 | 13.8 | 28.5 | 33.2 | 70.5 | - |
| | 1970 | | | | 33 | 47 | 97 | 170 | 238 | 285 | 382 |

## TABLE 4

### INCOME AFTER ALL TAXES AND BENEFITS AS A PERCENTAGE OF ORIGINAL INCOME*

| Ranges of Gross Income | | | | | | | | | | |
|---|---|---|---|---|---|---|---|---|---|---|
| | 1970 | £ 559- | 676- | 816- | 988- | 1196- | 1448- | 1752- | 2122- | Av. |
| | 1973 | £ 816- | 987- | 1194- | 1446- | 1749- | 2116- | 2561- | 3099- | Av. |
| 1 adult | 1970 | 84 | 77 | 71 | 68 | 60 | 61 | 56 | 65 | 74 |
| | 1973 | 85 | 83 | 78 | 72 | 69 | 68 | 69 | 63 | 80 |
| 2 adults + 2 children | 1970 | - | - | 117 | 93 | 89 | 84 | 81 | 81 | 83 |
| | 1973 | - | - | 96 | 100 | 93 | 88 | 84 | 83 | 86 |
| 2 adults + 3 children | 1970 | - | - | 128 | 112 | 104 | 98 | 90 | 91 | 92 |
| | 1973 | - | - | 118 | 120 | 108 | 102 | 96 | 91 | 96 |
| 2 adults + 4 children | 1970 | - | - | - | - | 120 | 105 | 102 | - | 108 |
| | 1973 | - | - | - | - | 126 | 114 | 107 | - | 112 |

*"equivalent" incomes, 1970 and 1973.

e) *Tax Relief on Mortgage Interest*

The main item that has contributed to the general increase in income after taxes and benefits is indirect benefits. These are housing subsidies, and are defined as the difference between current account expenditure by public authorities on housing and the rents paid by the tenants of local authority dwellings. This category limits itself to subsidies enjoyed by council house tenants and completely ignores the subsidy obtained by owner occupiers in the form of tax relief on mortgage payments. Council house tenants on average have lower incomes than owner occupiers, so that the present definition of indirect benefits introduces what is probably a spurious bias towards greater equality. Moreover, while the subsidies to council house tenants have increased substantially in recent years so, given the significant increase in the size of mortgages granted and in the level of building society interest rates, has the tax relief to owner occupiers.

Until such time as a realistic assessment of the indirect subsidies obtained by owner occupiers is included in the CSO analysis it may be advisable to drop the category indirect benefits.

The effect of excluding both indirect benefits and pensions on 'after tax and benefit' income is shown in Table 5.

Comparing Tables 4 and 5 it is clear that the exclusion of the two categories of benefit reduces the previous improvement in income after tax and benefit. This is particularly apparent for households comprising two adults and two children. The exclusion of pensions also reduces the deterioration in the lower income bands.

While these adjustments do not detract from the general improvement in the position of single adults and pensioners, it is apparent that once one gets beyond what are considered low earned incomes, there has been very little improvement for married couples with between one and three children. Moreover, it is clear that the CSO analysis is extremely sensitive to minor changes in definition. If there are benefits accruing to higher income households which are not recorded in the CSO analysis then its validity and usefulness is open to challenge.

f) *Other Fiscal Benefits*

The most obvious defect in the CSO analysis is that it largely ignores fiscal benefits. Tax relief on mortgages has already been mentioned as one instance of unrecorded subsidies. In addition there are a number of other allowances, tax exemptions and reliefs, such as those on life assurance and superannuation contributions which largely accrue to those with above average incomes.

Table 5

**INCOME AFTER ALL TAXES AND BENEFITS AS A PERCENTAGE OF ORIGINAL INCOME* EXCLUDING PENSIONS & DIRECT BENEFITS**

| *Ranges of Gross Income* | | | | | | | | | | |
|---|---|---|---|---|---|---|---|---|---|---|
| | 1970 £ | 559- | 676- | 816- | 988- | 1196- | 1448- | 1752- | 2122- | Av. |
| | 1973 £ | 816- | 987- | 1194- | 1446- | 1749- | 2116- | 2561- | 3099- | Av. |
| 1 adult | 1970 | 72 | 68 | 62 | 64 | 59 | 60 | 55 | 63 | 66 |
| | 1973 | 66 | 71 | 68 | 67 | 65 | 66 | 66 | 62 | 70 |
| 2 adults + | 1970 | - | - | 106 | 91 | 88 | 82 | 80 | 80 | 82 |
| 2 children | 1973 | - | - | 88 | 95 | 90 | 85 | 83 | 82 | 83 |
| 2 adults + | 1970 | - | - | 118 | 110 | 102 | 97 | 88 | 90 | 91 |
| 3 children | 1973 | - | - | 114 | 110 | 103 | 97 | 44 | 90 | 93 |
| 2 adults + | 1970 | - | - | - | - | 115 | 103 | 100 | - | 106 |
| 4 children | 1973 | - | - | - | - | 119 | 110 | 107 | - | 108 |

*"equivalent" incomes, 1970 and 1973.

There is some reflection of tax relief in the CSO analysis in that actual tax payments are recorded, but no account is taken of the notional tax liability of families if tax allowances did not exist. The nominally progressive nature of income tax and surtax is considerably reduced as the result of tax allowances, a tendency which is compounded by the inability of some low income families to fully utilise their tax allowances.

Tax concessions are a form of social welfare provision giving recognition to particular family needs. The absurd and iniquitous division between social welfare benefits and benefits accruing from the tax system can only be defended on the basis of administrative convenience. The basic inconsistency of the present CSO analysis is illustrated by the effect upon it of the introduction of negative income tax.

Under a negative income tax system cash payments would be made to those families who were unable to benefit to the full extent of their tax allowances. The present CSO analysis would treat the cash payments as a benefit while continuing to ignore tax allowances for higher income families. In other words only that half of a negative income tax regime which affected the lower incomes would be included in the CSO analysis, resulting in a spurious shift towards greater equality.

The treatment of fiscal subsidies in the CSO analysis leads to an overstatement of the egalitarian impact of taxation and benefits.

g) *Agricultural subsidies*

The proposal to include specific agricultural subsidies to the consumer, such as those on bread, butter and milk, as indirect benefits from 1974, is another example of how a misleading shift towards greater equality can be introduced into the CSO analysis.

The present treatment of agricultural subsidies is as follows:- "Agricultural subsidies are not treated as benefits to consumers. Such subsidies are included in the original income of farmers since they form part of the earnings of farmers who could otherwise earn comparable incomes in other employment."

The first sentence of this quotation is unexceptionable – indeed it would be completely misleading to treat general agricultural subsidies as benefits to consumers. Agricultural subsidies were designed to provide farmers with an "adequate" income, while allowing consumers to get the full benefit of low world prices. Thus, the subsidies only benefited farmers and not consumers. Furthermore it could be argued that the imposition of minimum import prices during the 1950s represented a hidden subsidy to farmers from consumers. Given expenditure patterns on food this hidden subsidy was undoubtedly regressive, but it is not recorded in the CSO analysis.

The second part of the quotation is false. There is ample evidence, both from the inter-war period and from the present plight of small hill farmers, to show that there are significant non-pecuniary benefits in farming which substantially offset monetary considerations alone. Subsidies paid to farmers provide cash over and above that needed to keep the majority of farmers in the industry.

The effect of agricultural subsidies is shown in Table 6. In 1969 direct exchequer support payments represented nearly 60% of farmers' net incomes. For specific types of farming this support sometimes represented all of a farmer's net income; moreover, as the size of the farm business increased, so did the proportion of net income represented by direct exchequer support. Agricultural subsidies are clearly regressive *within* the agricultural industry, the largest businesses obtaining the biggest subsidies. In 1969 these subsidies could add up to considerable amounts for the individual farmer. In 1969 a large livestock farmer received direct exchequer support amounting to £7,262. Certainly there is no logical reason why such subsidies should be treated differently from subsidies to low-income families.

**TABLE 6**

**DIRECT EXCHEQUER SUPPORT AS A PERCENTAGE OF NET FARM INCOME: ENGLAND & WALES 1969**

| | *Full-time farms by standard-man-day groups* | | | | | *Average* |
|---|---|---|---|---|---|---|
| | 275-599 | 600-1199 | 1200-1799 | 1800-2399 | 2400-4199 | 275-4199 |
| % of net income | 50 | 61 | 64 | 63 | 70 | 59 |

Source: T.E. Josling & D. Hamway

It has generally been recognised that the change-over from the deficiency payments system of agricultural support to that embodied in the Common Agricultural Policy was regressive. Josling and Hamway* estimated that "the net transfer from those earnings less than £36 a week is a formidable £504m" accruing to higher income families, and farmers (both continental and British). Admittedly the recent upsurge in world food prices has altered the basis of the estimate just quoted. However, this does not detract from the general point that the change in policy was regressive. The CSO analysis will only record those subsidies which

---

* T.E. Josling and Donna Hamway, "Distribution of Costs and Benefits of Farm Policy", in *Burdens and Benefits of Farm Support Policies*, Trade Policy Research Centre, 1972.

were introduced to alleviate the worst effects of the regressive shift in agricultural support policies.

h) *Other factors*

It is already clear that there are a number of factors which cast serious doubts upon the validity of any conclusions drawn from the CSO analysis. It is possible to enumerate a number of other defects in the CSO analysis, the majority of which lead to overstatement of the redistributive impact of taxes and benefits.

(i) The treatment of benefits such as education ignores the investment effect. Higher education in particular can and often does lead to higher earnings for the recipient. The majority of students at university still come from higher-income households and the education system may well be perpetuating, if not adding to, present inequality.

(ii) No account is taken of the quality of the education received. Urban schools which contain a predominance of children from lower income households often provide a poorer standard of education. Indeed equality of educational expenditure and staffing ratios may well imply a poorer standard of education. Higher expenditure and staffing ratios may be required in some urban schools to provide equality of educational benefit.

(iii) Differences in the treatment of employees and self-employed persons for tax purposes can disguise the true impact of taxation.

(iv) The imputed value of owner occupation is under-estimated. Webb and Sieve** estimated that the true figure "is over double the Government estimate for imputed rent."

(v) There is a general problem that the CSO analysis includes families with different sources of income and living in different types of housing in the same analysis. Given the small number of households in some of the more detailed breakdowns misleading fluctuations can arise.

(vi) No account is taken of capital gains. This applies both to owner-occupiers and to the option which higher income families have of either receiving income or opting for capital gains. (An example of the latter was shown in Section 4 of our evidence on Company Income.)

---

** A.L. Webb and J.E.B. Sieve, *Income Redistribution and the Welfare State*, Occasional Papers on Social Administration, No. 41 1971.

## *Concluding Comments*

The CSO analysis only shows a partial picture of the impact of taxation and benefits; one that may well lead to misleading conclusions. If the CSO analysis is to be continued it would be preferable for the sample size to be increased. Failing this an attempt should be made in the analyses to distinguish households by source of income and by type of dwelling.

Another approach would be to present analyses based upon alternative sets of assumptions. In this way various aspects of the impact of taxation and benefit policies could be more readily assessed. For cxample, estimates of educational benefits could be calculated on a cost basis, and on an investment value basis.

The CSO analysis should, henceforth, reflect the full value of tax reliefs. Otherwise it will remain nothing more than an interesting, but sterile, abstract exercise.

# 5

# Some Proposals for the Future

## *Actions in the near future*

Question 2b of the Standing Reference asks:

> "Is there any way in which any of these deficiencies can be removed or alleviated in the short term?".

Our purpose here is to discuss in general terms some possible remedies that could be set in motion relatively quickly. In particular we look at two types of question. Firstly, can existing single bodies of official data be analysed in new ways so as to shed more light on our subject? Secondly, could the bringing together of official data collected from various sources help us to get a much more adequate understanding of the make-up of the distribution and hence the type of actions necessary to secure "a fairer distribution of income and wealth"?

Single bodies of existing official data obviously could be analysed in many new ways. That the cost of so doing outweighs the extra benefit gained is the usual reason why they are not at present carried out. The benefit, however, is usually measured in relation to the specific purpose for which the data was originally collected whereas the Royal Commission is now concerned with the benefit in terms of shedding light on the distribution of income and wealth. It is quite to be expected, therefore, that new tabulations specifically designed for this new purpose will be needed. Moreover, given the promised help from the Government Statistical Service and the protection afforded to individual interests by the Royal Warrant there is every reason to expect them to take place. The outsider can often only get an imperfect idea of the details involved but I can suggest three types of new tabulation that would be helpful. Firstly, details could be obtained on the actual as distinct from nominal distribution of tax burdens as between people with different levels of gross income. Secondly, accounting periods of longer than one year could be examined. Thirdly, files on anonymous individuals could be built up as an alternative to the present reliance largely on grouped data. It might be helpful if we explain each of these ideas more fully.

### a) *Analyses of effective as well as nominal tax rates*

Retabulating the Inland Revenue data for a random sample of individual tax units would allow one to ascertain the actual burden of taxation in the 1970s on people at different levels in the gross income distribution. A special survey of a type similar to this was carried out by the Inland Revenue in 1959-60. It found that the top 5% of net incomes before tax secured proportionately far higher deductions or allowances for superannuation contributions, interest payments etc. than did lower ranges of income. And in the United States Pechman's work shows that the distinction between 'effective' and 'nominal' tax rates is important in ascertaining who actually bears the tax burden. Despite the clear need for such an exercise, however, recent official studies in the U.K. still rely on the far from satisfactory procedure of deducting on the basis of hypothetical tax rates. In Appendix M, 'The Effect of Tax on Salaries' of the Boyle Committee Report on Top Salaries, for example, it is assumed that tax is levied on all gross incomes apart from a deduction of a married man's personal allowance. On this basis it is no wonder that they conclude that 'the differentiations in gross salaries are very substantially reduced in terms of net income'. But we need to know with more certainty whether these people actually do pay this amount of tax.

### b) *Accounting periods of more than one year*

Our second suggestion also involves the Inland Revenue data, but this time it concerns the linking up of the records on an individual for more than one year. Once again the Inland Revenue has had no incentive to do this itself because tax is levied on annual incomes, but as the Commission recognise in their guidelines for submitting evidence, there is no necessary correlation between the distribution of annual income and the 'fairness' of the distribution. Soltow's work from tax returns in Norway, for example, shows that the distribution of lifetime incomes looks considerably different from that of annual incomes, and although the precise nature of his conclusions there may well not carry over to the U.K. there would seem to be strong grounds for our performing a similar exercise on a random sample of our population.

### c) *Construct files on anonymous individuals*

Our previous suggestion involved adding to our knowledge about the economic status of individuals, but this 'enrichment' concerned only the Inland Revenue data. Evidence from other surveys, such as the New Earnings Survey or General Household Survey, can also be retabulated in ways that shed more light on the nature and causes of individuals' positions. At present the Department of Employment present the earnings survey data grouped according to industry, occupation etc. and although there are a few bilateral cross-tabulations (e.g. earnings and hours) there is no attempt to put the individual at the centre of the analysis and to build up files on individuals and all of their characteristics at different levels in the distribution. Yet much more insight into the extent of the association between different variables and of the causes of inequality should be gained from doing this. Moreover, in the case of the general Household Survey one could have family and household files as well as individual ones and this would shed more light on important but neglected matters such as the extent to which relatively high-earning men and women team up in marriage. There is clearly much scope for the Commission to use these two bodies of data in new ways of this type for the specific purpose of facilitating greater public understanding of the nature of the distribution of income.

*d) Exercise in record-linking from different sources*

So far we have concentrated on what more could be done by each data collecting authority by itself. The potential gains possible if a combining of data from more than one source were possible are considerable too. The IR data does not have the age of the taxpayer, yet the systematic variation of income over the lifecycle would be better disentangled if age could be found out in each case. Similarly evidence from social security records could shed light on what happened to the taxpayer in years when his taxable income was not sufficient to raise him above the tax threshold and hence he did not appear on the IR files at all. In general the potential advantages from record linking are, and have been shown to be in other countries, very great indeed as far as shedding more light on the distribution of personal income. In the U.S., for example, Steinberg linked tax records with social security data and evidence from the 'Current Population Survey' for a sample of individuals in one year in the 1960s. And more recently Miller, David et al. in Wisconsin have linked records over an 18-year period and developed an Assets and Incomes Archive for 1946-64 which consists of eight basic data files.

*Longer-term proposal – an income question in the Population Census?*

Question 2d of the Standing Reference asks: "In the longer term is there any other way in which existing surveys can be modified to improve the statistics?". My purpose in this part of the Section is to critically examine the suggestion that one main way to improve the statistics on the distribution of income in the longer term is for an income question to be inserted into future population Censuses in Britain. The scope of the Census has increased considerably in the 1950s, 60s and 70s but there has been no successful move as yet to enable incomes to be analysed by size or in relation to other demographic characteristics on the basis of the data derived from this source. In short, despite the expanded scope of the Census there is still no income question in it. As a result it has been necessary to infer economic living standards from indirect indicators such as education, occupation and other dimensions of social status. Should the 1976 Census have an income question in it?

One line of argument in favour of an income question is that indirect measures are no adequate substitute for a direct question in incomes and there is indeed a real need to relate the answers to the income question to these other aspects so as to understand better the association of the inequality of incomes with them (Benjamin). More specifically, we do clearly need income information so as to compile our first reliable indicators of household income distributions according to location, and for disentangling the extent to which trends in income inequality over time reflect demographic factors such as the increase in the number of elderly persons living on their own whereas previously they resided with their sons and daughters. Neither of these specific questions can be comprehensively answered at present either by looking at each existing survey severally or by combining the information from each, whereas the insertion of an income question into the main census schedule of future population censuses in Britain would enable the first steps to be taken towards doing this in the longer term future.

In view of the need for an income question in the Census why therefore have we still not got one? There are in fact four main types of objection. Firstly, that other existing surveys which collect income data are sufficient in themselves without the need for the Census to look at income as well. Secondly, that other dimensions of social status, such as occupation, are a sufficiently good proxy for a direct measure of economic status for us to use the two interchangeably. Thirdly that the public is against the idea of an income question in the population census and that it would undermine the confidence in the other aspects of the census. Finally, that we already have a 1971 Census Income Follow-up which asked a 1% sample of the Census households to fill in a supplementary voluntary questionnaire in addition to the main census schedule. Let us look more closely at the validity of each of these main types of objections in turn.

The first argument is that existing sample surveys and official records with income data are sufficient. If we look at each of the main sources of evidence listed by the Royal Commission in its Guidelines for submitting evidence we can see that each one suffers defects compared to a population census with an income question in it. The Inland Revenue Surveys of Personal Incomes, for example, relate to tax units not individuals, families or households, and only to those tax units above the tax threshold at that. Clearly, this is not adequate for looking comprehensively at income inequality. The Family Expenditure Survey and the General Household Surveys do give social and demographic information along the same lines as the population Census, but unlike the Census they are based on such small samples that hardly any disaggregated analysis can be done, especially with respect to the important locational aspects of individuals. Suffice to say that the New Earnings Survey and the DHSS PAYE records deal only with earnings. Not one of the other sources therefore can come anywhere near matching the performance of a population census with an income question in it.

The second line of argument is that other aspects of social status, occupation for example, are good proxies for income. At the least this remains to be proved, but there are good grounds for believing that a thorough investigation of the association between social and economic status would reveal noticeable differences. Lydall, for example, looked at the extent to which the overall distribution of earnings can be explained by variations 'between' and 'within' occupations, and concluded that 'From these calculations we can conclude that not more than about 25% of the total variance of earnings is attributable to the variance between occupations'. And the General Register Office in its 1966 Classification of Occupations points out unequivocally that social class 'has no direct relationship to the average level of remuneration of particular occupations'. One cannot therefore, as has been done in the past, rely too heavily on indirect indicators of economic well-being instead of measuring it directly.

The third reason for not including an income question in future population Censuses is that the public at large is against it. While it is true that there is public antipathy to questions about income, such information is nevertheless required for a great number of purposes, such as house mortgages, educational grants, income tax etc., and questions on incomes are already asked in sample surveys such as the Family Expenditure Survey and the General Household Survey. Moreover, although it is true that the acceptability of a question on incomes was a major question before the 1971 Census and its field testing took up much of the 1968-9 pre-tests there were good reasons to believe that the pre-tests were not designed well and that the need for the information was not sufficiently well put across. Benjamin, for example, says that the responses were not satisfactory 'probably because exact amounts were asked for rather than classifications within a band'. And that although a subsequent survey in 1969 included a question in 'band' form, unfortunately the whole test suffered from adverse press comment. A far more determined attempt should therefore be made to make the public at large aware of the value and necessity of an income question in the population Census.

The final argument against is that we already have had a voluntary sample survey of incomes for 1% of the households enumerated in the Census which was carried out immediately after the main Census. This survey did, however, ask for exact amounts rather than bands of income and because it lacked the normal sanctions of the Census – compulsory response – the response rate was low. In any event a 1% sample is not large enough to provide sufficient cell numbers for detailed analyses by location. The Census-income follow-up is therefore not a satisfactory compromise solution to the problem.

An even more powerful positive argument in favour of collecting this new data is that America in the 1930s and 40s mirrors the dilemma that we in Britain are going through now about whether or not to put an income question in the population Census and in retrospect they are almost unanimously pleased that they did. It may be helpful for our choice therefore to look more closely at how things worked out in the U.S.

In the U.S. the 1940 Census collected income data for the first time. It did not however ask an exact or specific question, but rather it limited itself in the non-wage incomes part, for example, to asking, do you receive $50 or more a year? As a result only 2% failed to report their income. In 1950, using a 20% sample basis, a much more detailed income question was included, 20% of a Population Census sample still being very large compared to that used to collect data in the annual surveys, and sufficiently large to provide useful information for relatively small areas. 93% gave complete information and many of the non-respondents were away or sick rather than refusing to respond – Miller estimated that only 1% actually refused to answer the income question. In both 1940 and 1950 the income question was directed solely at individuals, particular ones at that – like the head of the household – but in 1960 a household basis was used and the sample was increased to 25%. Moving tentatively at first, therefore, the U.S. Census has been built into a very valuable source of information on the personal distribution of income. How did the public at large react to this development?

Miller is in no doubt. 'Today income information is regarded as one of the key facts collected in the Census. Indeed many people would not think of taking a census without collecting information about incomes. But that was not the case some thirty years ago'. In fact in 1940 the press and Congress exploded when it was first proposed that information on personal incomes should be collected in the Census. By 1960, however, there was no organised opposition at all. In short, 'what has emerged is one of the most useful bodies of income statistics ever collected' and in retrospect the public at large are well pleased that they took the plunge. This is not the place for a detailed discussion of how best to proceed in the UK, rather it has merely been our purpose to show that there is indeed a strong case for doing so, but the gradual development of income data in the Census appears to offer the best chance of success. The full-blooded pre-tests 1968-9 conducted in Britain failed as much because of the method adopted as anything else.

*References*

Boyle Committee (1974) *Report on Top Salaries* CMND 5846 (App.M)

Soltow, L. (1965) *Toward Income Equality in Norway* University of Wisconsin Press

Lydall (1968) *The Structure of Earnings* (page 104) Oxford University Press

David, M.H., Gates, W.A., and Miller, R.F. (1973) Linkage and *Retrieval of Microeconomic Data: A Report on the Wisconsin Assets and Incomes Archive*, Lexington Books

Miller, H.F. (1968) *Rich Man, Poor Man* (Appendix)

Miller, H.F. (1958) *The Income Data in the Decennial Population Census*

Benjamin, B. (1973) The 1971 Population Census and After *Journal of the Royal Statistical Society Series A*

Steinberg, J. (1970) 'Some Aspects of Statistical Data Linkage for Individuals' in Bisco, R.L. (Ed) *Data Bases, Computers and the Social Sciences*, Willey –.

Inland Revenue *Survey of Personal Incomes 1959-60* HMSO

Pechman, J.A. and Okner, B.A. (1972) 'Individual Income Tax erosion by income classes' in *The Economics of Federal Subsidy Programmes* (p. 13-40), General Study Papers (92 CONG. 2 SESS.)

# Appendix

## Equal Pay: A Critical Review of Progress

*Summary*

This Note combines recent data on women's employment published by the Department of Employment with earnings data from the New Earnings Survey.

1. The information on the number of women employed in specific industrial groups suggests that even if complete equality of pay is achieved there will still be a substantial male/female pay differential. All that would be gained is equality with low-paid men.

2. The structure of female activity rates indicates that women's pay will tend to lag behind that of men of the same age. Breaks in service can lead to restrictions on job and career prospects. Moreover, incremental scales in white-collar jobs ensure that interrupted service results in lower salary levels.

3. Data on basic rates of wages suggest that there has been some progress towards the elimination of discrimination. However, this often means that skilled women merely gain equality with low-paid men.

4. The male/female average earnings differential has tended to increase over the period 1948-69. Since then there has been a slight narrowing, to the extent that the relativity established in the latter half of the 1950's has been restored.

5. Shifts in male/female earnings differentials at various points in the distribution suggest that moves towards equal pay have not followed a uniform pattern. Indeed, male/female differentials based on wage rates do not appear to correlate with those derived from earnings.

6. Where unions actively seek to promote equal pay and ensure equal job opportunities there is scope for significant reductions in male/female earnings differentials.

*Conclusions*

The main conclusion is that even under an inadequate Equal Pay Act there is scope for unions to achieve a significant reduction in discrimination against women. In pursuing this unions need to carefully monitor changes in basic wage rates, earnings, types of payment system, job opportunities, and changes in incremental scales. Particular emphasis should be given by unions to that interpretation of equal pay implying 'equal pay for work of equal value'. Otherwise any realistic achievement of equal pay will be extremely difficult. Indeed there are so many loopholes in the present Equal Pay Act that, without vigorous action by trade unions, the attainment of equal pay can be compared to the pursuit of an elusive butterfly.

## Equal Pay: A Critical Review of Progress

*Introduction:*

In a previous Technical Note (No. 12: The Equal Pay Act 1970 – Interpretation and strategy for collective bargaining) a degree of scepticism was expressed about the effect the Equal Pay Act would have on differentials between men's and women's earnings. It was argued that progress towards the removal of the male/female wage rate and earnings differentials was "disappointingly small". Since that Technical Note was written a further two years of the five years allowed before the full implementation of the Equal Pay Act have elapsed, leaving barely twelve months until the Act is fully operative. Moreover, there is a proposal to introduce a Bill designed to complement the Equal Pay Act by making discrimination on the grounds of sex or marriage unlawful.* To a certain extent this proposed Bill will help to plug some of the gaps in the Equal Pay Act. However, if this new Bill passes through Parliament it will not become operative until the same date as the present Act – December 1975. Thus, the major part of any reduction in male/female pay differentials can be ascribed to the Equal Pay Act.

Although this Note is mainly concerned with changes in male/female earnings differentials, the way in which earnings are determined is a complex process which is subject to a variety of influences. Furthermore, the Equal Pay Act is primarily directed at basic rates of wages, and any reduction in the male/female wage differential may be offset by other factors. Thus, a general outline of some of the salient features of female employment and recent changes in women's wage rates will

---

* *Equality for Women: A policy for equal opportunity*, Cmnd 5724

be helpful in assessing changes in male/female earnings differentials.

The Department of Employment has recently published a number of booklets and articles on women and work.† The Department has also taken over the task, previously carried out by the office of Manpower Economics, of monitoring progress towards equal pay. In particular the Department of Employment has monitored changes in women's basic rates of wages. Thus a summary of some of the major points in the Department's publications provides a useful background to an assessment of changes in male/female earnings differentials.

*The Industrial distribution of female employees*

The distribution of female employees by major industrial groups is shown in Table 1. In June 1973 approximately 39 per cent of employees in employment were female. However, this overall figure disguises the fact that female employment is largely concentrated within a narrow range of industrial groups. With the exception of a few manufacturing industries which have traditionally employed large proportions of female labour, the bulk of female employment is confined to non-manufacturing industries. Thus over 73 per cent of female employees in employment were in non-manufacturing industries.+ Furthermore, approximately 55 per cent of women employees were covered by just three industrial groups – miscellaneous services, distributive trades, and professional and scientific services. A further two industrial groups – insurance, banking and finance, and public administration and defence – cover another 12 per cent of female employees. Thus, five out of twenty-seven industrial groups account for over two-thirds of female employment. (The equivalent proportion for men is just over one-third).

Recent trends in female employment have had the effect of reinforcing the concentration of female employment within a narrow group of industries. Indeed between 1959 and 1973 female employment in manufacturing industries fell by approximately 9 per cent, but this was more than offset by the growth of employment in the five industrial groups with the bulk of women workers.

The implication for moves towards equal pay of the highly uneven distribution of female employees is that it may be extremely difficult to alter the overall relationship between men and women's pay. Those

---

† Listed in Appendix

+ These figures disguise a much heavier concentration of non-manual females in non-manufacturing industries than manual.

industrial groups which cover the major part of female employment are those which contain a large proportion of low-paid men. Thus, even if complete equality of wage rates was achieved, let alone equality of earnings, this equality would mainly be with low-paid men. Equal pay between all men and women is thus partially dependent upon efforts to improve the relative position of low paid men.

*Female activity rates by age**

Figure 1 shows that after rising to a peak in the early twenties, female activity rates by age range declined during the late twenties. From thirty years of age there is a rapid increase in activity rates until the age range forty-five to fifty is reached; after this activity rates decline.

The obvious explanation for this pattern of activity rates is that after initial entry into the labour market many females leave, either upon marriage or when they have children. Young children below school age severely limit the ability of many women to remain in or enter the labour market. However, as children reach school age some of the barriers to employment are removed, and women enter or re-enter the labour force in increasing numbers.

The present age profile of female activity rates is a comparatively recent phenomenon, and is largely attributable to an increase in the employment of married women, a point which is illustrated in Figure 2. This shows that over the fifty years 1921 to 1971 there has been a marked increase in the activity rates of married women. In 1921 less than one in ten married women had jobs; by 1971 the proportion had risen to at least four in every ten.

A more detailed breakdown of female activity rates in recent years, together with forecasts for the future, has been compiled by the Department of Employment, and is reproduced here as Table 2. This shows that between 1951 and 1971 there was a substantial increase in the activity rates of married women in the thirty-five to fifty-nine age bracket, a trend which is forecast to continue into the immediate future. Indeed, increased activity rates by married women are a major element in future labour supply, as the major source for any growth is the size of the labour market.

The present age structure of female activity rates casts doubts as to whether equality of male and female pay can be achieved. The reason for this is that there are, particularly for white-collar workers, many cases where pay depends upon length of service. Thus, women who

* The proportion of females economically active

leave employment in their late twenties and return five to ten years later may find that they re-enter on the same scale point as they left. In the meantime their male counterparts have progressed several points up an incremental scale. Furthermore, a break from work can be detrimental to career and promotion prospects. The bearing of children and the looking after them in their earlier years can and often does imply that women will receive lower pay than men of equivalent age, even where equal pay is formally in force.

Quite apart from the fact that in some cases women re-entering the labour market cannot get back their old jobs and have to take lower-paid employment, the forecast increase in the activity of females in the age range thirty-five to fifty-nine indicates that interrupted employment will be an increasingly important contributor to the persistence of differentials between men and women's pay.

### *Wage Rates*

A major component of total earnings is basic rates of wages, and it is upon these that the Equal Pay Act will have a direct effect. The Department of Employment has monitored the moves towards equality of basic rates of wages, but mainly with reference to manual workers and to national agreements. It is thus difficult to assess the effect of the Equal Pay Act either on the wage rates of non-manual workers, or at plant and company level. However, even the comparatively restricted field covered by the Department of Employment's data does give some indication of progress towards equal pay.

A comparison between the annual increases in the indices of men's and women's hourly basic rates of wages is given in Table 3. This shows that there was a tendency for females to receive slightly greater increases in basic rates than men, the main exception being during the period April 1971 to April 1972, when the increases for men and women were of the same order. (Substantiating the qualms expressed about basic rates in the previous Technical Note).

The slight reduction in the differential does not imply that the actual cash differential between male and female rates declined, as may be illustrated by the following example. Assuming that female rates were 80% of the male rate of 100p an hour, the former is 80p per hour. Further assume a 15% increase in female rates and a 12% increase in male rates. Thus the new hourly rates are 112p for males and 92p for females. However, the cash differential between the male and female rates remains unchanged at 20p. Clearly while the percentage differential between male/female wage rates may have declined, the order of magnitude revealed in Table 3 is not enough necessarily to entail a reduction in the cash differential.

A more detailed analysis of changes in weekly rates of wages is shown in Tables 4, 5 and 6. Table 4 shows that there has been a fairly rapid narrowing of differentials between March 1970 and March 1974. The proportion of agreements and orders in which female rates as a percentage of male rates were 90% and over, rose from just over one twentieth in 1970 to nearly two-thirds in 1974.

Table 5 looks at the data from a slightly different angle. This shows that while one tenth of agreements eliminated discrimination against women, a similar proportion (11%) made no progress towards its elimination. Furthermore, while nearly a quarter of agreements or orders were eliminating discrimination as part of a phased plan, over half, while narrowing percentage differentials, were doing so on an ad hoc unplanned basis. Thus the main thrust towards the elimination of discrimination against women has resulted from a piecemeal process.

Table 6 gives an industrial breakdown of progress towards equal wage rates. This shows that the main impetus towards a narrowing of differentials took place in the distributive trades. Twelve of the sixteen agreements which eliminated discrimination were in this industrial group. Since a large proportion of women employees are to be found in the distributive trades, it would appear that there are grounds for believing that some progress has been made toward equal pay.

Before drawing too optimistic a conclusion from the partial elimination of wage rate discrimination against women, it is salutary to remember that even if equality of wage rates implied equality of earnings, equality with low paid men in distribution will do little to narrow the overall differential between male and female pay.

Moreover, the Department of Employment's data is largely concerned with the elimination of discrimination between the lowest paid men's and women's rates. Thus, skilled women may only get the same rate as unskilled men, and this is hardly a realistic definition of equal pay.

## *Earnings*

It has already been pointed out that the determination of earnings is an extremely complex matter, and is dependent upon a range of interrelated factors. One of the consequences of this is that earnings differentials between men and women can change independently of basic wage rates, and may offset the effects of the Equal Pay Act. Some of the factors which can effect the male/female earnings differentials are:

- differences in the amount of overtime worked and changes in its incidence;

- differences in the availability of payment by results and shift-work, together with changes in their incidence;
- alterations in the age at which the adult rate is payable;
- lengthening or shortening incremental scales, particularly if males and females are concentrated at different points on the scale;
- changes in promotion and training opportunities.

In such circumstances the measurement of progress towards equal pay is at best tentative, and needs to be supplemented by detailed information about each industry, agreement and job. However, despite these problems any meaningful concept of equal pay will seek to reduce unavoidable differentials between men's and women's earnings, and it is instructive to see what has happened to these during the initial stages of the Equal Pay Act. In order to do this the long-term (1948-73) relationship between men's and women's gross weekly earnings will be examined before moving on to a more detailed study of the recent past. The latter will look at changes in the relationship between average earnings by industrial group, by different points on the earnings distributions (both overall and for collective agreements), and according to the reduction in wage rate discrimination. Also, some of the other factors which can affect earnings differentials will be discussed.

*Long-term relationship*

Table 7 uses the Department of Employment's October Earnings Enquiry to show how the relationship between men's and women's earnings has changed over the period 1948 to 1973. Manual women's earnings as a percentage of manual men's have exhibited a tendency to deteriorate over the period since the end of World War II to the late 1960's. Since 1969 there has been a slight improvement in the relative position of women. This improvement is not particularly spectacular, and only restores the position which prevailed in the latter half of the 1950's.

The differential between non-manual men's and women's earnings has remained on a much more stable basis, with female earnings fluctuating around 53.5% of men's over the period 1959 to 1973.

From the evidence of Table 7 it appears that as far as moves towards equal pay are reflected in earnings there has been no change in the relative position of non-manual women, and only a marginal improvement for manual women. It can be argued that the data upon which Table 7 is based largely refer to manufacturing industries, and as such do not cover the effects of the main improvements in basic rates of wages which occur outside manufacturing. A more comprehensive industrial picture of changes in earnings for the period April 1970 to April 1974 is provided by the New Earnings Survey (N.E.S.).

*Changes in Average Earnings April 1970 - April 1974.*

Table 8 shows that the differential between the average weekly earnings of male and female manual workers in all industries and services has narrowed slightly over the period April 1970 to April 1974, (both including and excluding the effects of overtime). There seems little substance in the argument that non-manufacturing industries may have benefited disproportionately from a narrowing of wage rate differentials. Indeed, if anything, there is a slight tendency for females in non-manufacturing to have experienced a smaller improvement in their relative position than their counterparts in manufacturing.

Discounting the effects of overtime, there were considerable variations in the relationship between manual men's and women's earnings. While the overall position was an improvement of 4.4 percentage points, one industrial group, transport and communication, showed a deterioration, whilst another eight exhibited significant improvements:

foods, drink and tobacco;
other manufacturing industries;
mechanical engineering;
paper, printing and publishing;
electrical engineering.
professional and scientific services;
public administration;
vehicles;

Furthermore, despite the number of agreements which have removed wage rate discrimination against women in the distributive trades, this has not been reflected in earnings.

While the evidence of Tables 7 and 8 points to a reduction of inequality between male and female manual workers, there is no such correspondence between Tables 7 and 9, with regard to non-manual workers. Part of the reason for this is probably accounted for by differences in the dates of the two sets of data, but of greater importance is the broader coverage of non-manual workers by N.E.S. Table 9 shows that the improvement in non-manual females overall was slightly inferior to that of manual females. Also, as with manual workers, females in manufacturing fared marginally better than those in non-manufacturing.

On an industrial basis, the major improvements occurred in miscellaneous services, chemicals and allied industries, and electrical engineering. Clearly, apart from engineering, there is little correspondence between changes in the relative position of manual and non-manual females.

A major limitation of comparing averages, given that most of the effects of the Equal Pay Act are concentrated upon levelling women's rates to the lowest male rate, is that changes in averages may not fully reveal what has been happening at the lower end of the earnings distribution.

*Changes in medians, quartiles and deciles 1970-1974.*

Table 10 expresses manual and non-manual female workers' earnings distributions as percentages of the equivalent points on male workers' distributions.

For manual workers, on both an hourly and weekly basis, there is a tendency for females at the upper end of the earnings distribution to enjoy a greater improvement in their relative position than workers at the lower end. When non-manual workers are considered the pattern is reversed, those females at the lower end of the earnings distribution enjoying a greater improvement in their relative position than those at the top.

At this level of aggregation it is difficult to draw any firm conclusions. However, an insight into what is happening can be gained by looking at changes in the relative position of females covered by particular collective agreements or orders.

*Medians, quartiles and deciles, by collective agreement or order*

Tables 11, 12, and 13 present three different ways of looking at the relationship between different points on the male and female earnings distributions. Table 11 compares the relative positions in April 1970 and April 1974, on the basis of gross weekly earnings, while Table 12 expresses the relationships on the basis of gross hourly earnings. It can be argued that the relationships shown in these two tables are distorted by differences in the amount of overtime worked, and any changes therein. Unfortunately, no earnings distribution for men excluding the effect of overtime was published in 1970. Moreover, the N.E.S. does not publish the medians, quartiles and deciles of women's earnings excluding the effect of overtime. A possible way of partially overcoming the last point is to assume that there is little difference between the female earnings distributions whether or not overtime is included, and to use the former as a proxy for the latter. Table 13 shows points on the women's gross hourly earnings distribution as a percentage of equivalent points of the men's distribution, excluding overtime, both for April 1972 and April 1974.

From Tables 11, 12 and 13 it is clear that no distinct pattern emerges. In some cases (such as engineering) the top end of the female distribution has enjoyed a greater improvement in its relative position than the bottom end; in others (such as Local Authority, manual) the opposite is true. In a few cases (such as N.H.S. ancillary) all points on the distribution experienced changes of similar size. Furthermore, there are extreme cases where one end of the distribution has enjoyed an improvement in its relative position while the other suffered a deterioration.

*Rates of Wages and Earnings*

Table 14 relates the size of the reduction in the male/female wage rate differential, to the reduction in male/female earnings differentials according to the pattern and size of changes in relative position across the distribution. Thus for Local Authority manual workers, there was a reduction in the basic rates of wages male/female differential of over 20 percentage points; the largest improvements in relative earnings were at the lower end of the distribution; and the latter were over 20 percentage points. For Government industrial establishments, the reduction in the male/female rates of wages differential was between 11 and 20 percentage points; the reduction in the male/female earnings distribution was evenly spread throughout the distribution; and the latter was between 5 and 10 percentage points.

Table 14 illustrates the point that there is no direct relationship between the magnitude of a reduction in male/female rates of wages differential and the male/female earnings differential. While in some cases a reduction in the wage rate differential is reflected in a reduction in the earnings differential, at least over part of the earnings distribution, the exact relationship depends on a number of factors apart from changes in wage rates. The unions concerned with particular agreements will have a more intimate knowledge of these other factors; however, it is possible to make a few general observations.

1) A situation such as that in Engineering where minimal reduction in the wage rate differential was accompanied by a substantial reduction in the earnings differential at the top end of the earnings distribution is probably accounted for by the fact that no account has been taken of plant and company bargaining. While there has been little change in wage rate differentials at national level it may be that some of the larger companies covered by the national agreement have instituted company agreements which were more favourable to women.

2) Although most of the reduction in wage rate differentials has been reflected at the lowest decile of the Local Authority manual

workers distribution, the fact that its impact diminishes at higher points – unlike N.H.S. ancillary workers where the reduction in wage rate differentials has been felt at all points on the earnings distribution – suggests that most women in L.A. employment are concentrated in the lower grades, while in the N.H.S. they are more evenly distributed.

3) A similar concentration of women in the lower grades probably exists in retail distribution. Indeed, in one of the orders shown, Retail Drapery, the relative position of the highest decile decreased while that of the lowest decile increased. Such situations raise the possibility that the effects of moves towards equal pay are being offset by restrictions on female job opportunities, limiting women predominantly to low-paid unskilled jobs.

4) In the white collar agreements such as Local Authority general and clerical, Civil Service clerical grades, and teachers, where equal pay has existed for a number of years, the relationships between male and female earnings have not remained static. A major reason for this is probably reorganisation of salary structures and changes in the length of incremental scales. (The shifts within Local Authority, clerical and general would bear closer examination by the unions concerned.)

5) It is also interesting to note that despite the lack of any overt discrimination in terms of basic rates against women, the earnings of women were considerably less than men's. It is possible to postulate a number of reasons which would account for the continued existence of a male/female earnings differential, such as shorter or broken service restricting women to the lower points of incremental scales. In teaching part of the differential is undoubtedly due to the fact that there are higher proportions of women employed in primary than secondary schools. Another factor, closely linked with the previous two, is differences in promotion prospects. Thus, regardless of equality in basic rates there are forces which militate against equality of earnings.

### *Side effects and other factors*

In many agreements females were paid the adult rate at eighteen while males had to wait a further two or more years. One of the side effects of the Equal Pay Act is that there has been a move to set a common age for the payment of the adult rate. The usual practice has been to reduce the age at which the adult rate for *males* became payable to eighteen. Rather ironically the result of this has been to *increase* the gross weekly earnings male/female differential for manual workers. This is illustrated in Table 15, where average gross weekly earnings for manual females in the under eighteen range as a percentage of their male counterparts' *fell* by approximately 6 percentage points between 1970 and 1974. A similar but smaller drop occurred in the 18-20 age group. The main reason for this phenomenon is that male workers tend to work more overtime than female workers. Thus equalisation of basic rates where female rates were more advantageous implies an increase in the male/female earnings differential.

Table 15 also shows that the male/female earnings differential is largest in the age range 30 to 49 years. This is precisely the age range in which the activity rates of married women have increased most rapidly and from which it is forecast most of any future growth in the labour force will come. Obviously if this situation persists it will tend to retard any move to narrow the male/female earnings differential.

Two other factors which have an effect upon the male/female earnings differential are shiftwork and payment by results. On average the earnings of workers receiving these payments tend to be higher than those for the generality of workers. Clearly any imbalance between male and female workers with respect to the incidence of shiftwork and payment by results will lead to a male/female earnings differential. Furthermore, differential changes in the incidence of overtime or shiftwork will affect any attempt to eradicate discrimination against women. Thus, the fact that between 1970 and 1974 the proportion of women's earnings attributable to payment by results fell from 25.0 per cent to 15.8 per cent for women covered by the cotton and man-made fibres spinning and weaving agreement probably accounts for the general widening of the male/female earnings differential. (The equivalent percentages for men were 6.6 in 1970, and 5.3 in 1974). In any assessment of moves towards equal pay account must be taken of different payment systems and changes in their incidence.

*Concluding Comments*

Perhaps the most salient point to emerge from an assessment of the effects of the Equal Pay Act is that there can be no one simple panacea which will instantly eliminate pay discrimination against women. It is clear that the Equal Pay Act, which undoubtedly has had some influence on the removal of wage rate discrimination, is only a partial answer to the achievement of any comprehensive concept of equal pay.

It would be very easy to argue that little can be done about eliminating discrimination against women without a radical change in present social attitudes to the role of women in society. However, this is unnecessarily defeatist since there is scope for significant reductions in pay discrimination against women even under the aegis of the Equal Pay Act.

The Equal Pay Act leaves unresolved the hiatus between two concepts of equal pay: the T.U.C. and I.L.O.'s conviction that men and women should receive 'equal pay for work of equal value', and the narrower concept of 'equal remuneration for equal work'. As was stated in the previous Technical Note (No. 12), the "Equal Pay Act, 1970, far from clarifying this situation, in fact leaves room for either interpretation to be applied." Indeed, the analysis of earnings suggests this is precisely what has happened.

In some agreements, notably those for manual workers in the public sector, there has been a general and significant improvement in the relative position of all women. In others, such as the distributive trades, the main impact has been concentrated upon the lowest paid women This suggests that in the former there have been pressures to implement the broad 'equal pay for work of equal value' concept, while in the latter it is doubtful whether even the narrower concept of equal remuneration for equal work was being pursued, as opposed to mere minimum compliance with the Equal Pay Act, i.e. removal of overt discrimination against women by equating their basic rates with the lowest male rate. Furthermore, changes in the earnings distribution suggest that in some cases there may have been moves to restrict women to lower-paid jobs.

The situation discussed in the previous paragraph also casts light on the importance of trade union organisation. In the public sector there is a high degree of union organisation, while in the distributive trades union membership is much lower and Wages Councils are a major determinant of wages. Thus, a prerequisite for significant reductions in male/female pay differentials is a high degree of union penetration combined with union policies which make positive use of the flexibility of interpretation possible under the Equal Pay Act.

Trade unions can ensure that there is a significant reduction of male/female pay differentials within the agreements they are concerned with. In order to do this it is helpful if they:-

a) Ensure that the objective being aimed for is 'equal pay for work of equal value.'
b) Ensure that women are not confined to low graded jobs with little opportunity of moving to higher grades.
c) Ensure that females are not deprived of the opportunity to work under payment systems other than basic time rates.
d) Raise the relative position of low-paid men.
e) Ensure that female re-entrants are not discriminated against.

When monitoring progress towards equal pay there are a number of factors which trade unions should examine.

- changes in the incidence of overtime
- changes in the incidence of shiftwork
- changes in the incidence of payment by results
- changes in the relationship between men's and women's earnings at various points on their earnings distributions (including and excluding overtime)
- the impact of wage rate increases upon different points in the earnings distribution
- probable effect of plant and company agreements
- distribution of male and female employees by grade and occupation
- distribution of male and female employees along incremental scales.

**TABLE 1 EMPLOYEES IN EMPLOYMENT IN JUNE 1973 GREAT BRITAIN**

| *Industry Group* | *Numbers* | | *Females* | *Females as a percentage of* | *Growth in Female employment 1959-1973* |
|---|---|---|---|---|---|
| | Males | Females | All employees in each industry group | All females all industries and services | |
| | *(000s)* | *(000s)* | *per cent* | *per cent* | *(000s)* |
| Total all industries and services | 13,478 | 8,705 | 39.2 | 100.0 | + 1,546 |
| Total all manufacturing industries | 5,362 | 2,303 | 30.0 | 26.5 | - 188 |
| Agriculture, forestry etc. | 306 | 115 | 27.3 | 1.3 | - 29 |
| Mining and quarrying | 347 | 14 | 3.9 | 0.2 | - 7 |
| Food, drink and tobacco | 434 | 295 | 40.5 | 3.4 | - 16 |
| Coal and petroleum products | 36 | 4 | 10.0 | - } | - 10 |
| Chemicals and Allied industries | 302 | 123 | 28.9 | 1.4 } | 10 |
| Metal manufacture | 459 | 58 | 11.2 | 0.7 | - 9 |
| Mechanical Engineering | 806 | 150 | 15.7 | 1.7 } | |
| Instrument Engineering | 102 | 58 | 36.3 | 0.7 } | + 89 |
| Electrical Engineering | 478 | 318 | 39.9 | 3.7 } | |
| Shipbuilding and marine engineering | 165 | 12 | 6.8 | 0.1 | + 1 |
| Vehicles | 692 | 97 | 12.3 | 1.1 | - 18 |
| Metal goods not elsewhere specified | 397 | 166 | 29.5 | 1.9 | - 4 |
| Textiles | 299 | 256 | 46.1 | 2.9 | - 175 |
| Leather, leather goods and fur | 25 | 19 | 43.2 | 0.2 | - 5 |
| Clothing and footwear | 103 | 315 | 75.4 | 3.6 | - 55 |
| Bricks, pottery, glass, cement etc. | 234 | 65 | 21.7 | 0.7 | - 5 |
| Timber, furniture etc. | 231 | 55 | 19.2 | 0.6 | + 2 |
| Paper, printing and publishing | 382 | 185 | 32.6 | 2.1 | - 4 |
| Other manufacturing industries | 217 | 127 | 36.9 | 1.5 | + 23 |
| Construction | 1,244 | 94 | 7.0 | 1.1 | + 33 |
| Gas, electricity and water | 276 | 60 | 17.9 | 0.7 | + 20 |
| Transport and communication | 1,245 | 256 | 17.1 | 2.9 | + 33 |
| Distributive trades | 1,204 | 1,486 | 55.2 | 17.1 | + 171 |
| Insurance, banking, finance and business services | 503 | 540 | 51.8 | 6.2 | + 265 |
| Miscellaneous services | 943 | 1,171 | 55.4 | 13.5 | + 206 |
| Professional and scientific services | 1,055 | 2,115 | 66.7 | 24.3 | + 854 |
| Public administration and defence | 993 | 551 | 35.7 | 6.3 | + 188 |

Source: D of E Gazette August 1974.

TABLE 2 ACTIVITY RATES HISTORICAL AND PROJECTED. GREAT BRITAIN

| | | *1951* | *1961* | *1966* | *1971* | *1981* | *1986* | *1991* |
|---|---|---|---|---|---|---|---|---|
| 16-19* | Males | 98.8 | 98.3 | 98.1 | 98.8 | 98.8 | 98.8 | 98.8 |
| | Marries females | 38.1 | 41.1 | 43.9 | 42.4 | 42.4 | 42.4 | 42.4 |
| | Other females | 96.1 | 97.7 | 97.4 | 97.7 | 97.7 | 97.7 | 97.7 |
| 20-24* | Males | 98.7 | 97.3 | 98.5 | 98.8 | 98.8 | 98.8 | 98.8 |
| | Married females | 36.6 | 41.4 | 43.9 | 46.7 | 48.7 | 48.7 | 48.7 |
| | Other females | 94.3 | 95.3 | 95.4 | 94.4 | 94.4 | 94.4 | 94.4 |
| 25-34 | Males | 97.9 | 98.4 | 97.9 | 97.5 | 97.5 | 97.5 | 97.5 |
| | Married females | 24.4 | 29.5 | 34.3 | 38.4 | 41.7 | 43.3 | 44.3 |
| | Other females | 85.1 | 87.9 | 85.9 | 80.8 | 78.0 | 76.6 | 75.2 |
| 35-44 | Males | 98.6 | 98.8 | 98.4 | 98.3 | 98.3 | 98.3 | 98.3 |
| | Married females | 25.7 | 36.4 | 48.6 | 54.5 | 63.3 | 66.4 | 67.6 |
| | Other females | 77.0 | 81.7 | 82.5 | 80.0 | 78.8 | 78.2 | 77.6 |
| 15-54 | Males | 97.8 | 98.6 | 97.7 | 97.6 | 97.6 | 97.6 | 97.6 |
| | Married females | 23.7 | 35.3 | 49.8 | 57.0 | 68.2 | 73.2 | 75.0 |
| | Other females | 67.2 | 75.5 | 77.6 | 78.1 | 78.0 | 77.9 | 77.8 |
| 55-59 | Males | 95.0 | 97.1 | 95.4 | 95.3 | 95.3 | 95.3 | 95.3 |
| | Married females | 15.6 | 26.0 | 38.4 | 45.5 | 56.5 | 60.5 | 62.0 |
| | Other females | 50.9 | 63.1 | 66.6 | 67.2 | 65.9 | 65.3 | 64.7 |
| 60-64 | Males | 87.7 | 91.0 | 88.7 | 86.6 | 85.0 | 85.0 | 85.0 |
| | Married females | 7.2 | 12.7 | 21.3 | 25.2 | 31.6 | 33.2 | 34.2 |
| | Other females | 25.2 | 32.3 | 36.5 | 33.7 | 31.2 | 30.0 | 28.8 |
| 65-69 | Males | 47.7 | 39.9 | 37.3 | 30.6 | 25.0 | 23.0 | 22.0 |
| 70+ | Males | 20.3 | 15.2 | 14.0 | 11.0 | 9.0 | 8.0 | 7.5 |
| 65+ | Married females | 2.7 | 3.4 | 5.5 | 6.5 | 8.5 | 9.5 | 10.0 |
| | Other females | 6.4 | 6.9 | 7.4 | 6.3 | 6.1 | 6.0 | 5.9 |

Note: All historical data is based on census of Population estimates *Includes students as economically active

Source: D of E Gazette April 1974.

**TABLE 3**

**ANNUAL PERCENTAGE INCREASES IN BASIC HOURLY RATES OF WAGES: ALL INDUSTRIES AND SERVICES**

| | *Male* | *Female* |
|---|---|---|
| April 1970 - April 1971 | 12.3 | 15.8 |
| April 1971 - April 1972 | 11.7 | 11.4 |
| April 1972 - April 1973 | 15.4 | 18.6 |
| April 1973 - April 1974 | 12.3 | 16.4 |

**TABLE 4**

**LOWEST WOMEN'S RATES AS A PERCENTAGE OF LOWEST MEN'S NUMBER OF AGREEMENTS/ORDERS**

| *Percentage* | *March 1970* | *March 1972* | *March 1974* |
|---|---|---|---|
| 100 | - | 9 | 16 |
| 95-99 | 9 | 3 | 20 |
| 90-94 | | 12 | 61 |
| 85-89 | | 38 | 33 |
| | 34 | | |
| 80-84 | | 56 | 18 |
| Less than 80 | 123 | 48 | 9 |
| TOTAL | 166 | 166 | 157 |

(The difference between the totals at 1972 and 1974 represents collective agreements which became inoperative between the two dates).

**TABLE 5**

**COMPARISON OF DEPARTMENT OF EMPLOYMENT REGISTER AND INDEX OF MEN'S AND WOMEN'S RATES AT END-MARCH 1974**

| *Register category* | | *Percentage of women's to men's minimum rates at March 1974* | | | | | |
|---|---|---|---|---|---|---|---|
| | | 70 | 70-79 | 80-89 | 90-94 | 95-100 | Total |
| Discrimination removed | (V) | | | | | 16 | 16 |
| Phased plan | (W) | | | 5 | 20 | 12 | 37 |
| Larger increases | (X) | | 2 | 17 | 28 | 5 | 52 |
| Equal increases | (Y) | | 3 | 21 | 8 | 3 | 35 |
| No progress | (Z) | 2 | 2 | 8 | 5 | | 17 |
| TOTAL | | 2 | 7 | 51 | 61 | 36 | 157 |

Source: D of E Gazette August 1974

TABLE 6.
WOMEN'S RATES AS A PERCENTAGE OF MEN'S RATES IN COLLECTIVE AGREEMENTS AND WAGES ORDERS WHICH WERE DISCRIMINATORY IN MARCH 1970: MANUAL WORKERS: SUMMARY BY INDUSTRY GROUP

| *Industry Group* | *Number of agreements/ orders discriminating at January 1970* | *under 70 per cent* | *70-70 per cent* | *80-89 per cent* | *above 90 per cent* | *under 70 per cent* | *70-79 per cent* | *80-89 per cent* | *above 90 per cent* | *under 70 per cent* | *70-79 per cent* | *80-89 per cent* | *above 90 per cent* | *Number of agreement orders at end-March 1974* |
|---|---|---|---|---|---|---|---|---|---|---|---|---|---|---|
| Agriculture, forestry, etc. | 3 | | 2 | 1 | | | 1 | 2 | 2 | | | 2 | 1 | 3 |
| Mining and quarrying | | | | | | | | | | | | | | |
| Food, drink and tobacco | 18 | 2 | 15 | | 1 | | 6 | 11 | 1 | | 1 | 6 | 11 | 18 |
| Coal and petroleum products | | | | | | | | | | | | | | |
| Chemicals and allied industries | 10 | | 10 | | | | 3 | 7 | | | | 4 | 5 | 9 |
| Metal manufacture, all engineering & vehicles | 6 | | 2 | 4 | | | 2 | 3 | 1 | | | 1 | 3 | 4 |
| Metal goods | 11 | 3 | 3 | 4 | 1 | 3 | 1 | 5 | 2 | | 1 | 2 | 7 | 10 |
| Textiles | 23 | 10 | 12 | | 1 | 2 | 13 | 7 | 1 | | 4 | 8 | 9 | 21 |
| Leather, leather goods and fur | 4 | | 2 | 1 | 1 | | 1 | 2 | 1 | | | 1 | 3 | 4 |
| Clothing and footwear | 10 | 1 | 7 | 2 | | 1 | | 7 | 2 | | 1 | 7 | 2 | 10 |
| Bricks, pottery glass, etc. | 11 | | 5 | 6 | | | 2 | 9 | | | | 3 | 8 | 11 |
| Timber, furniture, etc. | 9 | | 6 | 3 | | | 4 | 5 | | | | 2 | 4 | 6 |
| Paper, printing & publishing | 12 | | 11 | 1 | | | 4 | 8 | | | | 7 | 5 | 12 |
| Other manufacturing | 5 | | 2 | 3 | | | 1 | 2 | 2 | | | | 5 | 5 |
| Construction | 2 | | | 1 | 1 | | | 1 | 1 | | | 1 | 1 | 2 |
| Gas, electricity, water | | | | | | | | | | | | | | |
| Transport & communication | 1 | | | | 1 | | | 1 | | | | | | |
| Distributive trades | 26 | 1 | 19 | 4 | 1 | 1 | | 15 | 9 | 1 | | 4 | 21 | 26 |
| Professional & scientific | 1 | | | | | | | 1 | | | | | 1 | 1 |
| Miscellaneous services | 9 | 1 | 5 | 2 | 1 | 1 | 2 | 5 | 1 | 1 | | 3 | 5 | 9 |
| Public administration | 6 | | 3 | 2 | 1 | | | 4 | 2 | | | | 6 | 6 |
| TOTAL | 167 | 18 | 105 | 34 | 9 | 8 | 40 | 94 | 24 | 2 | 7 | 51 | 97 | 157 |
| PER CENT OF TOTAL | 100 | 11 | 63 | 20 | 5 | 25 | 24 | 57 | 14 | 1 | 4 | 33 | 62 | 100 |

For details of wage rates chosen for comparison see table 4.

Source: D.E. Gazette August 1974.

TABLE 7.

**AVERAGE WEEKLY EARNINGS, BY SEX, AND FEMALE AS A PERCENTAGE OF MALE, 1948-73**

| *October* | *Full Time manual men age 21 & over* | *Full time manual women aged 18 or over* | *Column 2 as % of column 1* | *Non-manual males* | *Non-manual females* | *col.5 as % of col. 4.* |
|---|---|---|---|---|---|---|
| | £ | £ | % | £ | £ | % |
| 1948 | 6.90 | 3.71 | 53.8 | | | |
| 49 | 7.13 | 3.93 | 55.1 | | | |
| 50 | 7.52 | 4.12 | 54.8 | | | |
| 51 | 8.30 | 4.49 | 54.1 | | | |
| 52 | 8.93 | 4.81 | 53.9 | | | |
| 53 | 9.46 | 5.12 | 54.1 | | | |
| 54 | 10.22 | 5.41 | 52.9 | | | |
| 55 | 11.15 | 5.77 | 51.8 | | | |
| 56 | 11.90 | 6.16 | 51.8 | | | |
| 57 | 12.58 | 6.47 | 51.6 | | | |
| 58 | 12.83 | 6.70 | 52.2 | | | |
| 1959 | 13.54 | 7.05 | 52.1 | 18.03 | 9.65 | 53.5 |
| 60 | 14.53 | 7.42 | 51.1 | 19.10 | 10.13 | 53.1 |
| 1 | 15.34 | 7.73 | 50.4 | 20.04 | 10.68 | 53.3 |
| 2 | 15.86 | 8.04 | 50.7 | 21.13 | 11.35 | 53.7 |
| 3 | 16.75 | 8.41 | 50.2 | 22.25 | 11.97 | 53.8 |
| 4 | 18.11 | 8.95 | 49.4 | 23.53 | 12.60 | 53.6 |
| 5 | 19.59 | 9.60 | 49.0 | 25.53 | 13.71 | 53.7 |
| 6 | 20.30 | 10.07 | 49.6 | 26.69 | 14.25 | 53.4 |
| 7 | 21.38 | 10.56 | 49.4 | 27.90 | 14.90 | 53.4 |
| 8 | 23.00 | 11.30 | 49.1 | 29.77 | 15.76 | 52.9 |
| 1969 | 24.82 | 12.11 | 48.8 | 32.07 | 17.05 | 53.2 |
| 70 | 28.05 | 13.99 | 49.9 | 37.12 | 19.59 | 54.2 |
| 1 | 30.93 | 15.80 | 51.1 | 38.45* | 20.67* | 53.8 |
| 2 | 35.82 | 18.30 | 51.1 | 42.90* | 23.03* | 53.7 |
| 3 | 40.92 | 21.16 | 51.7 | 47.40* | 25.60* | 54.0 |

*Estimates

Source: Women and Work, a statistical survey, Department of Employment.

**TABLE 8**
**FEMALE EARNINGS AS A PERCENTAGE OF MALE, WEEKLY MANUAL WORKERS**

| | *Including overtime* | | | *Excluding overtime* | | |
|---|---|---|---|---|---|---|
| | *1970* | *1974* | *change* | *1970* | *1974* | *change* |
| All industries and services | 50.0 | 54.1 | 4.1 | 57.6 | 62.0 | 4.4 |
| All index of production industries | 50.0 | 53.2 | 3.2 | 57.7 | 60.8 | 3.1 |
| All manufacturing industries | 49.1 | 53.4 | 4.3 | 56.4 | 61.2 | 4.8 |
| All non-manufacturing industries | 49.8 | 53.7 | 3.9 | 57.4 | 61.3 | 3.9 |
| Food drink & tobacco | 50.2 | 55.9 | 5.7 | 59.1 | 67.0 | 7.9 |
| Chemicals & allied industries | 49.0 | 53.3 | 4.3 | 55.5 | 60.0 | 4.5 |
| Mechanical Engineering | 51.0 | 58.2 | 7.2 | 60.0 | 66.6 | 6.6 |
| Instrument Engineering | 54.4 | 58.0 | 3.6 | 60.8 | 64.6 | 3.8 |
| Electrical Engineering | 52.9 | 59.1 | 6.2 | 60.8 | 66.9 | 6.1 |
| Vehicles | 54.3 | 62.2 | 7.9 | 59.1 | 67.7 | 8.6 |
| Metal goods, n.e.s. | 48.1 | 51.5 | 3.4 | 56.4 | 60.4 | 4.0 |
| Textiles | 54.8 | 56.2 | 1.4 | 62.1 | 65.0 | 2.9 |
| Clothing & footwear | 57.4 | 58.2 | 0.8 | 60.9 | 62.9 | 2.0 |
| Bricks, pottery, glass cement etc. | 49.6 | 52.0 | 2.4 | 59.4 | 62.6 | 3.2 |
| Paper Printing & Publishing | 43.8 | 50.4 | 6.6 | 50.4 | 56.9 | 6.5 |
| Other manufacturing industries | 47.1 | 52.7 | 5.6 | 53.1 | 60.1 | 7.0 |
| Transport & communication | 69.1 | 67.8 | -1.3 | 77.7 | 75.3 | - 2.4 |
| Distributive trades | 52.4 | 56.6 | 4.2 | 59.0 | 63.1 | 4.1 |
| Professional & scientific services | 54.5 | 67.2 | 12.7 | 61.7 | 74.7 | 13.0 |
| Miscellaneous services | 50.7 | 56.9 | 6.2 | 55.8 | 61.2 | 5.4 |
| Public administration | 62.2 | 71.2 | 9.0 | 69.0 | 78.3 | 9.3 |

**TABLE 9**
**FEMALE EARNINGS AS A PERCENTAGE OF MALE, WEEKLY EXCLUDING OVERTIME NON-MANUAL WORKERS**

| | *1970* | *1974* | *Change* |
|---|---|---|---|
| All industries and services | 50.6 | 53.7 | 3.1 |
| All index of production industries | 44.5 | 48.5 | 4.0 |
| All manufacturing industries | 44.0 | 48.1 | 4.1 |
| All non-manufacturing industries | 52.7 | 54.8 | 2.1 |
| Chemicals and allied industries | 42.0 | 48.7 | 6.7 |
| Mechanical engineering | 44.9 | 47.1 | 2.2 |
| Electrical engineering | 43.2 | 49.5 | 6.3 |
| Vehicles | 46.8 | 51.2 | 4.4 |
| Gas, electricity and water | 50.0 | 54.3 | 4.3 |
| Transport and communication | 55.2 | 57.4 | 2.2 |
| Distributive trades | 42.5 | 47.3 | 4.8 |
| Insurance, banking and finance | 44.2 | 46.9 | 2.7 |
| Professional and scientific services | 59.3 | 59.7 | 0.4 |
| Miscellaneous services | 49.8 | 57.2 | 7.4 |
| Public administration | 58.5 | 61.6 | 3.1 |

**TABLE 10**

**OVERALL COMPARISON OF DISTRIBUTION**

| | *LD* | *LQ* | *M* | *HQ* | *HD* | *Av. weekly* |
|---|---|---|---|---|---|---|
| | *Manual women's earnings as a percentage of manual men's;* | | | | | |
| 1970 | 51.2 | 51.0 | 50.0 | 49.2 | 49.1 | 50.0 |
| 1 | 53.1 | 53.0 | 52.0 | 51.3 | 50.7 | 52.0 |
| 2 | 53.3 | 52.9 | 52.4 | 52.0 | 52.1 | 52.1 |
| 3 | 53.3 | 52.7 | 51.6 | 51.5 | 51.3 | 51.7 |
| 4 | 54.7 | 54.7 | 54.3 | 53.8 | 53.9 | 54.1 |
| | *Non-manual women's earnings as a percentage of non-manual men's* | | | | | |
| 1970 | 52.6 | 51.2 | 50.6 | 50.1 | 50.2 | 49.7 |
| 1 | 55.2 | 54.0 | 52.3 | 51.2 | 51.0 | 50.6 |
| 2 | 54.4 | 53.4 | 52.2 | 51.5 | 51.5 | 51.0 |
| 3 | 55.3 | 53.8 | 52.1 | 51.3 | 51.1 | 51.4 |
| 4 | 59.4 | 55.1 | 53.8 | 52.9 | 50.1 | 52.6 |
| | *Manual women's earnings as a percentage of manual men's: hourly* | | | | | |
| 1970 | | | | | | |
| 0 | 60.4 | 60.1 | 58.8 | 57.1 | 57.1 | 58.8 |
| 1 | 60.6 | 61.8 | 60.1 | 58.5 | 57.8 | 59.8 |
| 2 | 61.0 | 62.2 | 60.6 | 59.1 | 59.1 | 60.4 |
| 2 | 60.3 | 62.2 | 60.5 | 59.3 | 59.3 | 60.3 |
| 3 | 61.0 | 61.7 | 61.1 | 59.8 | 59.5 | 60.7 |
| 4 | 62.7 | 64.4 | 63.8 | 62.6 | 62.1 | 63.4 |
| | *Non-manual women's earnings as a percentage of non-manual men's: hourly* | | | | | |
| 1970 | | | | | | |
| 0 | 54.5 | 54.4 | 53.2 | 51.3 | 52.2 | 52.6 |
| 1 | 57.1 | 56.0 | 54.2 | 52.6 | 53.1 | 53.4 |
| 2 | 56.0 | 55.3 | 54.5 | 53.2 | 54.4 | 54.1 |
| 2 | 56.0 | 55.3 | 54.5 | 53.3 | 54.4 | 54.1 |
| 3 | 57.4 | 56.1 | 54.1 | 52.8 | 54.7 | 54.4 |
| 4 | 59.4 | 57.7 | 56.6 | 54.4 | 55.0 | 55.8 |

Note; There was a change in the basis from which hourly earnings were calculated in 1972.

**TABLE 11**
**WOMEN'S GROSS WEEKLY EARNINGS AS A PERCENTAGE OF MEN'S (1)**

| *Private sector* | | *Lowest decile* | *Lower quartile* | *Median* | *Upper quartile* | *Highest decile* |
|---|---|---|---|---|---|---|
| Engineering – manual (U.K.) | 70 | 59.5 | 55.6 | 52.3 | 49.3 | 49.1 |
| | 74 | 61.4 | 60.1 | 57.2 | 57.0 | 57.4 |
| | change | 1.9 | 4.5 | 4.9 | 7.7 | 8.3 |
| Food manufacturing JIC (GB) | 70 | 53.5 | 50.5 | 49.2 | 48.3 | 47.7 |
| | 74 | 62.8 | 61.7 | 58.8 | 53.7 | 48.3 |
| | change | 9.3 | 11.2 | 9.6 | 5.4 | 0.6 |
| Printing and book-binding (E & W. except London) | 70 | 56.7 | 51.2 | 48.3 | 43.9 | 42.6 |
| | 74 | 64.3 | 59.1 | 55.6 | 52.8 | 51.8 |
| | change | 7.6 | 7.9 | 7.3 | 8.9 | 9.2 |
| Cotton and man-made fibre spinning & weaving | 70 | 75.0 | 66.7 | 66.5 | 66.8 | 66.0 |
| | 74 | 69.6 | 64.2 | 60.5 | 63.4 | 63.3 |
| | change | - 5.4 | - 2.5 | - 6.0 | - 3.4 | - 2.7 |
| Hosiery & knitwear NJIC (Midlands) | 70 | 57.3 | 53.2 | 53.4 | 53.2 | 53.9 |
| | 74 | 55.2 | 61.6 | 53.9 | 56.5 | 62.0 |
| | change | - 2.1 | 8.4 | 0.5 | 3.3 | 8.1 |
| Woollen & worsted spinning and weaving (Yorkshire) | 70 | 60.0 | 54.6 | 57.1 | 57.8 | 58.1 |
| | 74 | 65.6 | 57.4 | 53.3 | 55.9 | 52.6 |
| | change | 5.6 | 2.8 | - 3.8 | - 1.9 | - 5.5 |
| Footwear manufacture (U.K.) | 70 | 64.6 | 61.0 | 62.5 | 64.0 | 61 7 |
| | 74 | 66.8 | 63.9 | 61.0 | 62.4 | 67.1 |
| | change | 2.2 | 2.9 | - 1.5 | - 1.6 | 5.4 |
| Retail co-operative societies (G.B.) | 70 | 61.0 | 54.6 | 50.5 | 47.4 | 46.7 |
| | 74 | 65.6 | 60.2 | 55.0 | 53.8 | 52.0 |
| | change | 4.6 | 5.6 | 4.5 | 6.4 | 5.3 |
| Retail multiple grocery and provisions (E & W) | 70 | 51.0 | 52.9 | 49.3 | 46.0 | 46.9 |
| | 74 | 57.7 | 55.1 | 50.8 | 45.3 | 40.2 |
| | change | 6.7 | 2.2 | 1.5 | - 0.7 | - 6.7 |

| *Public sector* | | *Lowest decile* | *Lower quartile* | *Median* | *Upper quartile* | *Highest decile* |
|---|---|---|---|---|---|---|
| Local Authorities (E & W) - general & clerical division | 70 | 67.7 | 73.4 | 77.2 | 76.6 | 75.7 |
| | 74 | 76.0 | 78.1 | 83.3 | 78.3 | 70.5 |
| | change | 8.3 | 4.7 | 6.1 | 1.7 | - 5.2 |
| Local Authorities (E & W) - manual | 70 | 54.9 | 54.2 | 54.3 | 55.0 | 60.5 |
| | 74 | 70.0 | 66.1 | 64.7 | 64.3 | 65.2 |
| | change | 15.1 | 11.9 | 10.4 | 9.3 | 4.7 |
| Civil Service – clerical | 70 | 85.6 | 84.6 | 79.5 | 87.5 | 89.1 |
| | 74 | 89.5 | 86.3 | 86.2 | 91.4 | 90.4 |
| | change | 3.9 | 1.7 | 6.7 | 3.9 | 1.3 |
| Government industrial establishments | 70 | 71.8 | 66.7 | 60.9 | 56.0 | 56.8 |
| | 74 | 81.9 | 73.3 | 70.2 | 65.6 | 62.1 |
| | change | 10.1 | 6.6 | 9.3 | 9.6 | 5.3 |
| National Health Service – ancillary | 70 | 65.2 | 63.6 | 62.1 | 57.7 | 55.7 |
| | 74 | 78.1 | 77.0 | 73.6 | 69.5 | 71.1 |
| | change | 12.9 | 13.4 | 11.5 | 11.8 | 15.4 |
| Teachers in primary and secondary schools (E & W) | 70 | 85.8 | 76.2 | 77.9 | 86.0 | 85.6 |
| | 74 | 87.5 | 81.7 | 78.5 | 84.0 | 85.1 |
| | change | 1.7 | 5.5 | 0.6 | - 2.0 | - 0.5 |
| *Wages Councils* | | | | | | |
| Licensed residential establishments (GB) | 70 | 68.6 | 61.9 | 61.4 | 57.5 | 53.0 |
| | 74 | 77.4 | 74.9 | 64.6 | 58.0 | 51.7 |
| | change | 8.8 | 13.0 | 3.2 | 0.5 | - 1.3 |
| Retail drapery etc. (GB) | 70 | 60.5 | 58.5 | 56.9 | 57.5 | 56.9 |
| | 74 | 70.2 | 63.4 | 59.2 | 57.3 | 54.0 |
| | change | 9.7 | 4.9 | 2.3 | - 0.2 | - 2.9 |
| Retail food trades (E & W) | 70 | 54.7 | 53.1 | 51.0 | 47.9 | 46.9 |
| | 74 | 59.7 | 59.4 | 55.0 | 53.1 | 47.0 |
| | change | 5.0 | 6.3 | 4.0 | 5.2 | 0.1 |
| Retail furnishing etc. (GB) | 70 | 57.6 | 54.4 | 52.9 | 49.1 | 46.4 |
| | 74 | 65.7 | 62.4 | 55.8 | 51.3 | 51.1 |
| | change | 8.1 | 8.0 | 2.9 | 2.2 | 4.7 |

(1) The N.E.S. is a sample survey and as such the published figures are subject to standard errors. These standard errors are larger at the deciles and quartiles than at the median, e.g. a percentage standard error of 1 at the median is approximately associated with percentage standard errors of 1.1 at the quartiles and 1.4 at the deciles.

**TABLE 12**
**WOMEN'S GROSS HOURLY EARNINGS AS A PERCENTAGE OF MEN'S (1)**

| *Private sector* | | *Lowest decile* | *Lower quartile* | *Median* | *Upper quartile* | *Highest decile* |
|---|---|---|---|---|---|---|
| Engineering – manual (U.K.) | 70 | 67.1 | 62.8 | 59.5 | 55.9 | 54.2 |
| | 74 | 68.7 | 67.2 | 64.8 | 63.8 | 64.4 |
| | change | 1.6 | 4.4 | 5.3 | 7.9 | 10.2 |
| Food manufacturing JIC (GB) | 70 | 63.5 | 63.4 | 58.8 | 59.3 | 64.8 |
| | 74 | 73.8 | 72.3 | 70.1 | 67.7 | 62.4 |
| | change | 10.3 | 8.9 | 11.3 | 8.4 | - 2.4 |
| **Printing & bookbinding (E & W except London)** | 70 | 60.0 | 57.0 | 54.5 | 51.3 | 49.2 |
| | 74 | 70.7 | 63.0 | 61.3 | 59.0 | 56.5 |
| | change | 10.7 | 6.2 | 6.8 | 7.7 | 7.3 |
| Cotton & man-made fibres spinning & weaving | 70 | 82.5 | 79.5 | 76.4 | 73.0 | 73.9 |
| | 74 | 78.6 | 72.8 | 67.0 | 72.5 | 75.5 |
| | change | - 3.9 | - 6.7 | - 9.4 | - 0.5 | 1.6 |
| Hosiery & knitwear NJIC (Midlands) | 70 | 61.7 | 60.4 | 58.7 | 58.3 | 61.3 |
| | 74 | 64.5 | 67.5 | 59.9 | 62.8 | 70.2 |
| | change | 2.8 | 7.1 | 1.2 | 4.5 | 8.9 |
| Woollen & worsted spinning & weaving (Yorkshire) | 70 | 69.2 | 66.7 | 69.2 | 65.8 | 67.2 |
| | 74 | 75.3 | 71.3 | 67.1 | 64.3 | 64.4 |
| | change | 6.1 | 4.6 | - 2.1 | - 1.5 | - 2.8 |
| Footwear manufacture (U.K.) | 70 | 71.8 | 65.7 | 67.8 | 68.3 | 69.8 |
| | 74 | 74.9 | 70.2 | 64.1 | 66.0 | 72.7 |
| | change | 3.1 | 4.5 | - 3.7 | - 2.3 | 2.9 |
| Retail Co-operative societies (GB) | 70 | 64.8 | 60.5 | 59.1 | 58.7 | 56.7 |
| | 74 | 72.2 | 66.7 | 62.8 | 67.3 | 58.6 |
| | change | 7.4 | 6.2 | 3.7 | 8.6 | 1.9 |
| Retail multiple grocery and provisions (E & W) | 70 | 60.0 | 56.8 | 55.0 | 48.7 | 50.7 |
| | 74 | 63.2 | 61.1 | 55.1 | 49.7 | 49.0 |
| | change | 3.2 | 4.3 | 0.1 | 1.0 | - 1.7 |
| *Public Sector* | | | | | | |
| Local authorities (E & W) general & clerical division | 70 | 66.7 | 72.3 | 79.7 | 81.8 | 82.9 |
| | 74 | 76.3 | 81.1 | 84.1 | 81.2 | 71.9 |
| | change | 9.6 | 8.8 | 4.4 | - 0.6 | -11.0 |

| | | *Lowest decile* | *Lower quartile* | *Median* | *Upper quartile* | *Highest decile* |
|---|---|---|---|---|---|---|
| Local Authorities (E & W) manual | 70 | 65.3 | 65.8 | 65.9 | 66.7 | 71.8 |
| | 74 | 85.6 | 81.7 | 78.0 | 76.9 | 77.8 |
| | change | 20.3 | 15.9 | 12.1 | 10.2 | 6.0 |
| Civil Service – clerical | 70 | 85.9 | 84.7 | 80.8 | 89.3 | 92.3 |
| | 74 | 88.6 | 87.2 | 87.7 | 92.7 | 93.8 |
| | change | 2.7 | 2.5 | 6.9 | 3.4 | 1.5 |
| Government industrial establishments | 70 | 75.7 | 71.3 | 66.3 | 65.1 | 64.0 |
| | 74 | 84.3 | 78.2 | 74.9 | 73.7 | 73.9 |
| | change | 8.6 | 6.9 | 8.6 | 8.6 | 9.9 |
| National Health Service – ancillary | 70 | 70.7 | 69.5 | 67.7 | 67.0 | 69.8 |
| | 74 | 87.5 | 84.4 | 83.0 | 82.5 | 85.4 |
| | change | 16.8 | 14.9 | 15.3 | 15.5 | 15.6 |
| Teachers in primary and secondary schools (E & W) | 70 | 85.3 | 76.8 | 79.0 | 84.4 | 85.3 |
| | 74 | 88.1 | 83.2 | 78.9 | 84.3 | 85.2 |
| | change | 2.8 | 6.4 | - 0.1 | - 0.1 | - 0.1 |
| *Wages Councils* | | | | | | |
| Licenced residential establishments (GB) | 70 | 71.4 | 70.7 | 67.6 | 63.9 | 61.1 |
| | 74 | 84.8 | 82.0 | 72.9 | 62.1 | 55.4 |
| | change | 13.4 | 11.3 | 5.3 | - 1.8 | - 5.7 |
| Retail drapery, etc. (GB) | 70 | 64.4 | 62.4 | 60.4 | 59.4 | 59.3 |
| | 74 | 72.8 | 67.3 | 61.8 | 60.0 | 54.2 |
| | change | 8.4 | 4.9 | 1.4 | 0.6 | - 5.1 |
| Retail food trades (E & W) | 70 | 60.6 | 60.0 | 56.4 | 52.1 | 49.7 |
| | 74 | 69.1 | 66.4 | 59.4 | 54.4 | 50.6 |
| | change | 8.5 | 6.4 | 3.0 | 2.3 | 0.9 |
| Retail furnishing etc. (GB) | 70 | 61.6 | 59.5 | 57.6 | 54.0 | 51.6 |
| | 74 | 69.8 | 66.8 | 60.5 | 55.9 | 55.5 |
| | change | 8.2 | 7.3 | 2.9 | 1.9 | 3.9 |

See note to Table 11.

**TABLE 13**

**WOMEN'S GROSS HOURLY EARNINGS AS A PERCENTAGE OF MEN'S (MEN'S EARNINGS EXCLUDE OVERTIME)**

| | | *Lowest decile* | *Lower quartile* | *Median* | *Upper quartile* | *Highest decile* |
|---|---|---|---|---|---|---|
| *Private sector* | | | | | | |
| Engineeeing – manual (UK) | 72 | 67.2 | 65.4 | 63.2 | 60.5 | 59.4 |
| | 74 | 71.9 | 69.7 | 66.7 | 64.9 | 65.0 |
| | change | 4.7 | 4.3 | 3.5 | 4.4 | 5.5 |
| Food manufacturing JIC (GB) | 72 | 68.4 | 70.9 | 69.7 | 65.8 | 61.5 |
| | 74 | 79.8 | 77.6 | 74.3 | 71.4 | 63.9 |
| | change | 11.4 | 6.7 | 4.6 | 5.6 | 2.4 |
| Printing & book-binding (E & W except London) | 72 | 65.5 | 62.0 | 58.3 | 54.0 | 51.7 |
| | 74 | 73.6 | 66.2 | 64.6 | 61.0 | 58.6 |
| | change | 8.1 | 4.2 | 6.3 | 7.0 | 6.9 |
| Cotton & man made fibres spinning & weaving | 72 | 83.7 | 82.3 | 73.4 | 71.8 | 71.5 |
| | 74 | 83.8 | 78.9 | 71.0 | 74.9 | 76.6 |
| | change | 0.1 | - 3.4 | - 2.4 | 3.1 | 5.1 |
| Hosiery & knitwear NJIC (Midlands) | 72 | 65.2 | 65.3 | 59.5 | 59.8 | 61.8 |
| | 74 | 66.3 | 68.6 | 59.4 | 63.1 | 69.6 |
| | change | 1.1 | 3.3 | - 0.1 | 3.3 | 7.8 |
| Woollen & worsted spinning & weaving (Yorkshire) | 72 | 69.0 | 64.7 | 66.8 | 64.4 | 63.7 |
| | 74 | 77.0 | 74.4 | 69.0 | 66.2 | 66.0 |
| | change | 8.0 | 9.7 | 2.2 | 1.8 | 2.3 |
| Footwear manufacture (U.K.) | 72 | 75.4 | 67.3 | 64.6 | 68.9 | 68.3 |
| | 74 | 75.8 | 72.0 | 61.9 | 66.9 | 72.7 |
| | change | 0.4 | 4.7 | - 2.7 | 2.0 | 4.4 |
| Retail Co-operative Societies (GB) | 72 | 64.9 | 73.1 | 67.4 | 66.1 | 59.9 |
| | 74 | 74.7 | 70.3 | 65.8 | 68.7 | 58.7 |
| | change | 9.8 | - 2.8 | - 1.6 | 2.6 | - 1.2 |

**TABLE 13 (cont'd)**

| | | *Lowest decile* | *Lower quartile* | *Median* | *Upper quartile* | *Highest decile* |
|---|---|---|---|---|---|---|
| Banking | 72 | 64.3 | 55.1 | 52.1 | 49.1 | 46.7 |
| | 74 | 66.5 | 61.5 | 59.3 | 54.1 | 49.1 |
| | change | 2.2 | 6.4 | 7.2 | 5.0 | 2.4 |
| *Public Sector* | | | | | | |
| Local Authorities (E & W) – general & clerical | 72 | 81.9 | 79.3 | 81.9 | 84.3 | 86.7 |
| | 74 | 76.6 | 81.1 | 84.1 | 81.4 | 79.1 |
| | change | - 5.3 | 1.8 | 2.2 | - 2.9 | -14.8 |
| Local Authorities ( E & W) – manual | 72 | 73.8 | 74.1 | 75.6 | 74.5 | 77.1 |
| | 74 | 86.9 | 84.5 | 80.5 | 78.3 | 78.8 |
| | change | 13.1 | 10.4 | 4.9 | 3.8 | 1.7 |
| Local Authorities (E & W) – | | | | | | |
| Civil Service – clerical | 72 | 84.1 | 87.1 | 84.3 | 88.0 | 90.7 |
| | 74 | 88.7 | 88.4 | 88.5 | 93.5 | 94.3 |
| | change | 4.6 | 1.3 | 4.2 | 5.5 | 3.6 |
| Government industrial establishments | 72 | 86.1 | 78.2 | 74.5 | 69.0 | 66.4 |
| | 74 | 87.6 | 81.5 | 77.8 | 75.5 | 75.3 |
| | change | 1.5 | 3.3 | 3.3 | 6.5 | 8.9 |
| *Public Sector* | | | | | | |
| National Health Service ancillary | 72 | 78.8 | 78.1 | 77.4 | 75.3 | 77.7 |
| | 74 | 90.5 | 87.3 | 85.0 | 84.5 | 86.7 |
| | change | 11.7 | 9.2 | 7.6 | 9.2 | 9.0 |
| Teaching (E & W) | 72 | 86.6 | 80.4 | 78.0 | 85.1 | 85.3 |
| Primary & Secondary | 74 | 88.1 | 83.1 | 78.9 | 84.3 | 85.2 |
| Schools | change | 1.5 | 2.7 | 0.9 | - 0.8 | - 0.1 |
| *Wages Councils* | | | | | | |
| Licensed residential | 72 | 76.7 | 72.5 | 67.7 | 61.9 | 61.9 |
| establishments (GB) | 74 | 88.0 | 84.4 | 74.5 | 62.4 | 55.8 |
| | change | 11.3 | 11.9 | 6.8 | 0.5 | - 6.1 |
| Retail bread | 72 | 56.5 | 57.5 | 61.0 | 58.0 | 53.8 |
| | 74 | 65.8 | 65.7 | 61.8 | 58.5 | 64.0 |
| | change | 9.3 | 8.2 | 0.8 | 0.5 | 10.2 |

TABLE 13 (cont.)

| | | *Lowest decile* | *Lower quartile* | *Median* | *Upper quartile* | *Highest decile* |
|---|---|---|---|---|---|---|
| Retail drapery etc. (GB) | 72 | 67.5 | 64.7 | 61.4 | 59.8 | 54.5 |
| | 74 | 73.5 | 68.2 | 62.1 | 60.3 | 54.2 |
| | change | 6.0 | 3.5 | 0.7 | 0.5 | - 0.3 |
| Retail food trades (E & W) | 72 | 63.7 | 65.5 | 62.2 | 56.5 | 51.3 |
| | 74 | 70.4 | 67.9 | 60.0 | 55.5 | 50.9 |
| | change | 6.7 | 2.4 | - 2.2 | - 1.1 | 0.4 |
| Retail furnishing | 72 | 61.6 | 61.9 | 59.7 | 52.9 | 48.1 |
| | 74 | 70.3 | 67.5 | 61.4 | 56.0 | 55.5 |
| | change | 8.7 | 5.6 | 1.7 | 3.1 | 7.4 |

The N.E.S. is a sample survey and as such the published figures are subject to standard errors. These standard errors are larger at the deciles and quartiles than at the median, e.g. a percentage standard error of 1 at the median is approximately associated with percentage standard errors of 1.1 at the quartiles and 1.4 at the deciles.

TABLE 14.

**THE RELATIONSHIP BETWEEN CHANGES IN BASIC RATES OF WAGES AND EARNINGS; BY SIZE OF CHANGE AND BY EFFECT ON DIFFERENT POINTS ON THE EARNINGS DISTRIBUTION; APRIL 70 - APRIL 74.**

| *Reduction in male/female wage rate differential.* | | *Change in male/ female earnings differential along the distribution (1)* | *Magnitude of the reduction in male/female earnings differential (at its greatest point) (2)* |
|---|---|---|---|
| Over 20 percentage points and over:- | | | |
| Retail Co-operative Societies | (23) | O | 4 |
| Retail multiple grocery and provisions | (25) | P | 5 |
| Woollen and worsted spinning and weaving (Yorkshire) | (23) | P | 4 |
| Retail finishing etc. | (23) | P | 4 |
| Local Authority (E & W) manual | (21) | P | 1 |
| Food manufacturing industry (GB) | (21) | P | 3 |

**TABLE 14 (cont.)**

| *Reduction in male/female wage rate differential* | | *Change in male/ female earnings differential along the distribution* (1) | *Magnitude of the reduction in male/female earnings differential (at its greatest point) (2)* |
|---|---|---|---|
| 15 and under 20 percentage points:- | | | |
| Retail Food trades (E & W) | (16) | P | 4 |
| Retail drapery etc. (GB) | (15) | P | 4 |
| Government industrial establishments | (15) | E | 4 |
| N.H.S. ancillary | (15) | E | 2 |
| 10 and under 15 percentage points:- | | | |
| Printing and bookbinding (E & W except London) | (12) | O | 3 |
| Licensed residential establishments (GB) | (12) | P | 3 |
| 1 and under 10 percentage points:- | | | |
| Cotton and man-made fibres etc, | ( 5) | N | 5 |
| Footwear manufacturing | ( 7) | O | 5 |
| Engineering – manual (U.K.) | ( 1) | N | 3 |
| No change:- | | | |
| Local Authority – general and clerical | | P | 4 |
| Civil Service – clerical | | O | 4 |
| Teaching | | P | 4 |

(1) P = tendency for the lower end of the earnings distribution to operate greater increases than the top.
N = tendency for the upper end of the earnings distribution to experience greater increases than the bottom.
E = tendency for all points on the earnings distribution to get equal increases.
O = other patterns of earnings increase.

(2) 1 = 20 percentage points and over increase.
2 = 15 and under 20 percentage point increase.
3 = 10 and under 15 percentage points increase.
4 = 5 and under 10 percentage points increase.
5 = under 5 percentage points increase.

TABLE 15

**a) WOMEN'S EARNINGS AS A PERCENTAGE OF MEN'S BY AGE APRIL 1974**

| | *Manual* | | | *Non-Manual* | | |
|---|---|---|---|---|---|---|
| | inc. overtime | excl. overtime | excl. o/time | inc. overtime | excl. overtime | excl. overtime |
| | weekly | | hourly | weekly | | hourly |
| Under 18 | 90.9 | 97.1 | 99.3 | 92.7 | 94.3 | 96.4 |
| 18 to 20 | 72.3 | 80.0 | 81.0 | 83.2 | 85.8 | 86.7 |
| 21 to 24 | 59.0 | 66.9 | 68.2 | 73.9 | 75.7 | 78.2 |
| 25 to 29 | 55.0 | 62.8 | 64.6 | 63.2 | 64.9 | 67.2 |
| 30 to 39 | 50.7 | 58.6 | 61.6 | 54.3 | 55.5 | 57.9 |
| 40 to 49 | 52.9 | 61.2 | 64.1 | 49.8 | 50.8 | 52.4 |
| 50 to 59 | 56.1 | 64.2 | 66.2 | 54.7 | 55.7 | 57.8 |
| 60 to 64 | 56.6 | 63.0 | 66.9 | | | |
| All ages | | | 65.6 | | | 55.8 |

**b) WOMEN'S EARNINGS AS A % OF MEN'S BY AGE APRIL 1970**

| | | |
|---|---|---|
| under 18 | 96.8 | 89.0 |
| 18 to 20 | 69.5 | 82.2 |
| 21 to 24 | 57.3 | 69.9 |
| 25 to 29 | 51.4 | 62.5 |
| 30 to 39 | 48.3 | 52.4 |
| 40 to 49 | 48.2 | 48.6 |
| 50 to 59 | 51.0 | 52.1 |
| 60 to 64 | 52.3 | - |
| All ages | 51.2 | 49.7 |

Source: N.E.S. 1970 and 1974.

**WHEN MARRIED WOMEN GO OUT TO WORK**

**FIGURE 1.** *Percentage of total economically active by age-group, 1971*

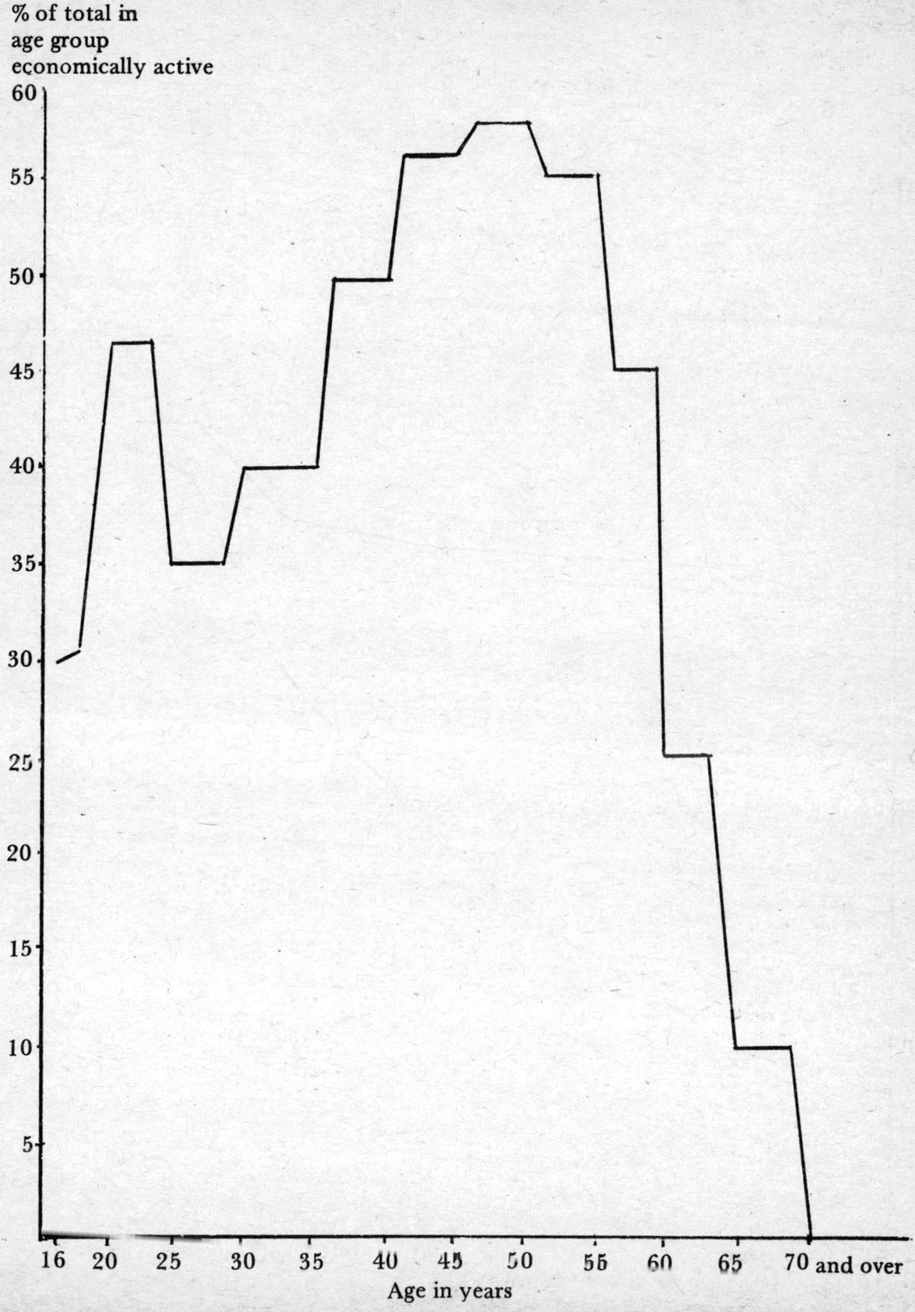

**WOMEN AT WORK 1921-71**

**FIGURE 2.** *Percentage going out to work*

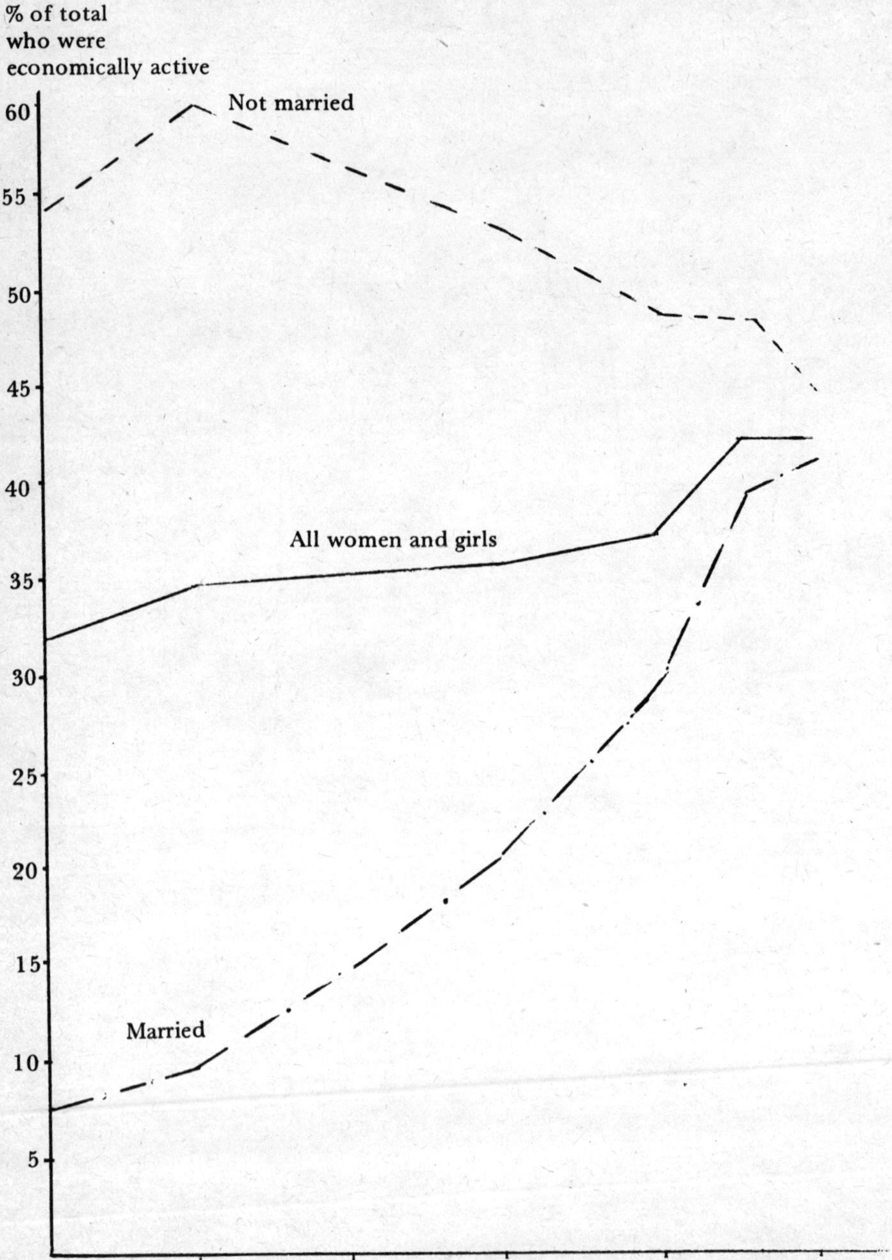

## APPENDIX

The Department of Employment has recently published several articles and publications which bear on equal pay.

*Manpower papers*

| | |
|---|---|
| No. 9 | Women & Work: a statistical survey |
| No. 10 | Women & Work: sex differences and society |
| No. 11 | Women & Work: a review |
| No. 12 | Women & Work: overseas practice |

*D.E. Gazette*

| | |
|---|---|
| January 1974 | Female activity rates, p. 8. |
| April 1974 | Labour force projections 1973-1991, p.304. |
| August 1974 | Progress towards equal pay, p. 691. |
| November 1974 | Working women, p. 982. |